# Roald Dahl

Twayne's English Authors Series
*Children's Literature*

James H. Gellert, Editor
*Lakehead University*

TEAS 492

ROALD DAHL
(1916–1990)
*Courtesy of Viking Press*

# Roald Dahl

## Mark I. West
*University of North Carolina at Charlotte*

Twayne Publishers • New York
Maxwell Macmillan Canada • Toronto
Maxwell Macmillan International • New York   Oxford   Singapore   Sydney

823
Dahl

*Roald Dahl*
Mark I. West

Twayne Publishers
Macmillan Publishing Company
866 Third Avenue
New York, New York 10022

Maxwell Macmillan Canada, Inc.
1200 Eglinton Avenue East
Suite 200
Don Mills, Ontario M3C 3N1

Macmillan Publishing Company is part of the Maxwell Communication Group of Companies.

**Library of Congress Cataloging-in-Publication Data**

West, Mark I.
  Roald Dahl / Mark I. West.
      p.       cm. — (Twayne's English authors series ; TEAS
  492. Children's literature)
  Includes bibliographical references (p. 139) and index.
  ISBN 0-8057-7019-4
  1. Dahl, Roald—Criticism and interpretation.   I. Title.
  II. Series: Twayne's English authors series ; TEAS 492.
  III. Series: Twayne's English authors series. Children's literature.
  PR6054.A35Z94    1992
  823'.914—dc20                                                        91-33737
                                                                            CIP

10 9 8 7 6 5 4 3 2 1

Printed in the United States of America

*To my parents,*
*Carolyn and Walter West*

# Contents

# Preface

Roald Dahl is a difficult author to label. He grew up in Great Britain and lived there for much of his life, which is why he is included in Twayne's English Authors Series. A case could be made, however, that he should be seen as an American author. He began his writing career in America in the early 1940s, and for a long time his stories and books appeared in America before they came out in England. It was not until the mid-1970s that Dahl began giving his English publishers the chance to bring out the first editions of his works.

Another reason he defies pigeonholing is that he achieved tremendous success both as an author of adult stories and as an author of children's books. He first became famous for his macabre short stories for adults. During the 1940s, 1950s, and 1960s these stories regularly ran in the *New Yorker,* the *Atlantic Monthly, Playboy,* and several other major American magazines. They also appeared in three highly praised collections: *Someone Like You* (1953), *Kiss Kiss* (1960), and *Switch Bitch* (1974).

Dahl began his career as a children's author in the early 1960s. His first children's book, *James and the Giant Peach,* came out in 1961 and was followed by *Charlie and the Chocolate Factory* in 1964. These two books became so popular that Dahl would have been known as an important children's author even if these were his only children's books, but they actually proved to be but the first of a long string of books. Following the publication of *Charlie and the Chocolate Factory,* Dahl wrote 17 other books for children, including such best-sellers as *Danny, the Champion of the World* (1975), *The BFG* (1982), *The Witches* (1983), and *Matilda* (1988).

The two major divisions in Dahl's writing career have led to similar divisions in the criticism of his works. Some critics have studied his adult stories, and others have studied his children's books, but until now no one has examined his entire canon. This book is the first serious attempt to analyze both aspects of Dahl's writing career. Nearly everything that Dahl wrote is covered in this book; the only exceptions are some of the short stories that do not appear in Dahl's major collections. This comprehensive approach reveals an interesting pattern. In almost all of Dahl's fiction—whether it be intended for children or for adults—authoritarian figures, social institutions, and societal norms are ridiculed or at least undermined.

Although not a biography, this book does include much biographical information. The connections between Dahl's life and his work are many, and a number of these connections are examined at various points in this book. In researching Dahl's life I received significant help from the ultimate authority on the subject, Dahl himself. Dahl kindly allowed me to conduct a lengthy interview with him at his home in Great Missenden, England. During the interview he provided me with valuable information about his writing career, and much of this material is included in these pages. Dahl also read the biographical chapter for factual accuracy. Although his death has made it impossible for me to thank him properly, I remain grateful for his willingness to help me.

My appreciation also goes to the Southern Regional Education Board, which made it financially possible for me to go to Great Missenden; to Malcolm Usery, who helped me solve a particularly thorny research problem; to James Gellert, who first encouraged me to write this book and served as my initial editor; and to Regina Hayes and Cara Garofalo, who gave me access to the manuscripts of Dahl's final children's books. I am especially thankful to my wife, Nancy Northcott, who provided me with much encouragement and advice.

# Chronology

**1954**  Purchases farmhouse in Great Missenden, England. Daughter Olivia Twenty born 20 April. Wins Edgar Allan Poe Award.

**1957**  Daughter Tessa born 11 April.

**1959**  Wins second Edgar Allan Poe Award.

**1960**  *Kiss Kiss*. Son, Theo Matthew Roald, born 30 July.

**1961**  *James and the Giant Peach*.

**1962**  Daughter Olivia dies 17 November.

**1964**  Daughter Ophelia Magdalena born 12 May. *Charlie and the Chocolate Factory*.

**1965**  Patricia Neal suffers massive stroke, 17 February. Daughter Lucy Neal born 4 August.

**1966**  *The Magic Finger*.

**1970**  *Fantastic Mr. Fox*.

**1972**  *Charlie and the Great Glass Elevator*.

**1974**  *Switch Bitch*.

**1975**  *Danny, the Champion of the World*.

**1979**  *My Uncle Oswald*. Separates from Patricia Neal.

**1982**  *The BFG*.

**1983**  *The Witches*. Divorces Patricia Neal and marries Felicity Crosland. Wins Whitbread Award.

**1984**  *Boy: Tales of Childhood*.

**1986**  *Going Solo*.

**1988**  *Matilda*.

**1990**  Dies 23 November in Oxford, England.

# 1

# Charting His Own Course

When Lewis Nichols, a columnist for the *New York Times Book Review,* heard the advance publicity for Roald Dahl's *James and the Giant Peach,* he immediately took notice. Why, he wondered, would Dahl, "a specialist in the eerie, macabre, chiller-type story," write a children's book? Positing an answer to his own question, Nichols theorized that Dahl wanted to take a "sabbatical" from "probing the eerie for adults."[1] Time, however, has proven Nichols wrong. Rather than simply taking a temporary departure from his career as an adult author, Dahl was launching a second career as a children's author. Following the publication of *James and the Giant Peach* in 1961, Dahl wrote numerous children's books, including the immensely popular *Charlie and the Chocolate Factory.* He also, though, continued to write short stories for adults.

In the face of Dahl's ability to write for two widely different audiences, many critics tend to view him as a kind of two-headed creature. Nichols, for example, called the adult's Dahl "bitter" and the child's Dahl "sweet" (Nichols, 8). When questioned about this tendency, Dahl dismissed it. "It's a mistake," he said, "to see me as two different people. I'm not"[2] He is, of course, right. Even though there are major differences between his often frightening short stories for adults and his humorous books for children, they are products of the same mind. A careful reader can see signs of Dahl's distinct mind-set in practically everything he has written. It is the mind-set of an outsider—one who distrusts not only society's authority figures but also the socializing process in general. As one would expect, the formation of this mind-set began in Dahl's childhood.

## Childhood and Schooling

Although Dahl was born in Wales, both of his parents came from Norway. His father, Harald Dahl, immigrated to South Wales around the turn of the century and helped establish the successful shipbrokering firm of Aadnesen and Dahl in the busy port city of Cardiff. Not long after the death of his first wife, he took a trip back to Norway in the hope of finding a woman who would marry him and help him raise his young son and daughter. There he met Sofie Magdalene Hesselberg, whom he married in 1911. The couple moved to Dahl's home in Llandaff, a village outside Cardiff. Over the next six years they had five children, including Roald, who was born on 13 September 1916. In 1920 Harald Dahl died, leaving his wife with a sizable estate, as well as with instructions to send their children to English schools.

The circumstances surrounding Roald Dahl's early years helped make him into an outsider. He grew up feeling stronger ties to Norway than to England. Around the house his mother spoke mostly Norwegian, and her children all learned the language. She also read them Norse myths and legends and took them on annual trips to Norway to visit relatives. Some of the happiest moments in Roald Dahl's childhood occurred during these prolonged visits. Just as his warm feelings toward Norway stemmed from his mother's love of the country, his feelings of detachment from England were also influenced by his mother. Unlike her husband, she had often felt estranged in her adopted country. In fact, if not for her husband's desire to have their children educated in English schools, she might have moved the family to Norway after his death. She dealt with her feelings of estrangement by focusing her energies on raising her children. As a result Roald Dahl grew up in a happy and close-knit family, but one that was rather isolated from the surrounding society.

Ironically, the British educational system so admired by Harald Dahl succeeded in crushing much of the happiness that characterized his son's early childhood. This process had much to do with the schools' frequent use of severe corporal punishment, a practice Roald Dahl's mother neither engaged in nor condoned. Dahl first encountered corporal punishment while attending a preparatory school, the Llandaff Cathedral School. He and some of his classmates played a boyish prank on a local shopkeeper. They were caught, and the headmaster beat them with a cane. When Dahl's mother noticed the welts on his buttocks, she complained to the headmaster. He responded by calling her a foreigner and arguing that she "didn't understand how British schools were run."[3] This incident prompted her to enroll Dahl in an English boarding school called St. Peter's in the hope that he would be treated more kindly there.

Located across the Bristol Channel from Cardiff, St. Peter's was not far from Dahl's home, but when he arrived there in September 1925 he felt as if he had entered an alien world. Like most English boarding schools of that period, St. Peter's relied on regimentation, humiliation, and frequent canings to keep the boys in line. While this approach was not much liked by any of the boys, it especially upset Dahl, for it completely contradicted the way in which he had been raised. From the very first day, he hated the school and longed to return to the family fold. Whenever he went to bed, he made sure that he was facing in the direction of his home. On one occasion he even faked the symptoms of appendicitis in order to be sent home for a few days. Dahl's feelings of alienation carried over into his academic performance. He did not excel in any of his classes, and he did quite poorly in Latin.

Dahl's only positive learning experiences at St. Peter's occurred on Saturday mornings. This was when the school's regular teachers went to a local pub for two and a half hours and left the students in the care of a woman named Mrs. O'Connor. Although hired as a babysitter, she took it upon herself to teach the boys about English literature. She gave the students a booklet containing a chronological listing of major events in the literary history of England, and each week she gave a talk about one of these events. As Dahl later recalled, her talks sparked his lifelong interest in literature:

> She had the great teacher's knack of making everything she spoke about come alive to us in that room. In two and a half hours, we grew to love Langland and his Piers Plowman. The next Saturday, it was Chaucer, and we loved him, too. Even rather difficult fellows like Milton and Dryden and Pope all became thrilling when Mrs. O'Connor told us about their lives and read parts of their work to us aloud. And the result of all this, for me at any rate, was that by the age of thirteen I had become intensely aware of the vast heritage of literature that had been built up in England over the centuries. I also became an avid and insatiable reader of good writing. . . . Perhaps it was worth going to that awful school simply to experience the joy of her Saturday mornings.[4]

In September 1929 Dahl began attending Repton, one of the most prestigious schools in England. Dahl selected the school on his own, but he ended up disliking it nearly as much as St. Peter's, as he quickly found himself in conflict with the school's rules and traditions. Repton insisted that its students wear an elaborate uniform, and Dahl resented this requirement. He also resented the traditional power that the older students had over their younger schoolmates. These older students, known at Repton as Boazers, made all sorts of ridiculous demands on the younger boys and beat them if they did not obey. One Boazer, for example, ordered Dahl to make his morning toast. Another insisted that Dahl sit on the toilet seat before the Boazer used it so that it would be warm. Dahl's reactions to such practices differed significantly from the reactions of most of his classmates. Rather than look forward to the day when he would be a powerful Boazer, he simply rejected the whole tradition.

Continuing the pattern he started at St. Peter's, Dahl did not do well in most of the classes that he took at Repton. One of his worst subjects was English composition. In 1930 his composition teacher wrote, "I never met a boy who so persistently writes the exact opposite of what he means. He seems incapable of marshalling his thoughts on paper" (*Wonderful*, 187). His composition teacher for the summer term of 1932 was even harsher, criticizing Dahl's character as well as his academic performance. "This boy," the teacher charged, "is an indolent and illiterate member of the class" (*Wonderful*, 188).

With one or two exceptions, Dahl thought as little of his teachers as they thought of him. He especially disliked the headmaster, a clergyman who took sadistic pleasure in flogging the students. It struck Dahl as strange for a clergyman to preach about mercy and forgiveness and then to beat a boy so severely that a sponge and basin were required to clean up the blood. This type of hypocrisy caused Dahl to question much more than the moral authority of his teachers. As he wrote many years later, he began "to have doubts about religion and even about God. If this person, I kept telling myself, was one of God's chosen salesmen on earth, then there must be something very wrong about the whole business" (*Boy*, 132).

Not all of Dahl's experiences at Repton were negative, but his pleasures usually had little to do with his classwork. One of his favorite activities was taste-testing chocolates for Cadbury, the famous candy manufacturer. The company occasionally asked the students to rate samples of new chocolate bars, a task that Dahl performed with "great gusto" (*Boy*, 133). He also acquired a passion for photography. He built his own darkroom, learned how to develop negatives, and even had an exhibition of his photographs. Another source of joy for Dahl was sports. He became exceptionally good at Eton-fives, a game similar to handball, and was named captain of the school team. As a captain, Dahl enjoyed a certain amount of status among his classmates, and this helped to make his life at Repton more bearable.

While in his final year at Repton, Dahl decided not to attend college, even though his mother offered to send him to Oxford or

Cambridge. He had come to think of formal education as a stifling ordeal, and he wanted nothing more to do with it. What he wanted was to have adventures and visit faraway places, and he set out to find a job that would help him achieve that goal. He applied to several companies that did international business, but he had his heart set on working in one of the foreign branches of the Shell Oil Company. Shortly before graduating from Repton he interviewed with Shell, and they offered him a position in their London office, with the assurance that he would be transferred to one of their foreign branches after he completed his training and reached the age of 21. He happily accepted the position and reported to work in September 1934. Although he enjoyed his prolonged training period, he continually looked forward to receiving his foreign assignment. The moment he had been waiting for finally arrived in 1938. He was summoned into the office of a company director, who told him to prepare for a three-year stint in East Africa.

## Africa and the Royal Air Force

Dahl's entire family assembled on the London Docks to see him off as he set out on his long trek to Dar es Salaam, a coastal town in Tanganyika, part of what is now known as Tanzania. Shell owned a house in the town, and Dahl took up residence there along with two other Shell employees. He spent his first two months studying Swahili and learning the details of Shell's operations in East Africa. Soon thereafter he began taking the company's station wagon on month-long trips to visit the mines and plantations that made up the bulk of Shell's customers in the region. These trips took him into remote parts of Africa where the roads were little more than ruts and the wildlife roamed openly. Every day on the road offered its own adventures, and Dahl found it all quite exhilarating.

Aside from occasional encounters with poisonous snakes and a bout with malaria, Dahl thoroughly enjoyed his life in Africa. He liked learning the language and the customs of the native people and became close friends with the Mwanumwezi tribesman who served as his assistant. The wild animals, tropical climate, and beautiful scenery also appealed to him. But perhaps most of all he liked his newfound independence. For the first time in his life he was free to disregard the standards and conventions of English society. Remembering this period, he wrote, "I loved it all. There were no furled umbrellas, no bowler hats, no sombre grey suits and I never once had to get on a train or a bus."[5] This experience helped to crystallize his outsider mind-set, for he now realized that there were other ways to live and other ways to view the world.

Dahl's idyllic days came to an abrupt halt when England declared war on Germany in September 1939. At the time Tanganyika was a British territory, but it had once been in German hands, and many Germans still lived in Dar es Salaam. The British officials in the town feared that these Germans might stage an uprising, so they made plans to round up the German males and hold them in a prison camp. In order to carry out this plan, they needed more military officers. They therefore made all of the young Englishmen in the town temporary officers in the King's African Rifles. Dahl suddenly found himself in command of 25 African soldiers. He was ordered to block the main road leading out of Dar es Salaam and turn back any Germans who attempted to escape. Although Dahl had a hard time thinking of these neighbors as enemies, he obeyed his orders and set up the blockade. He was eventually involved in a violent confrontation with a group of Germans, who, as anticipated, attempted to flee. The leader of this group grabbed Dahl and attempted to take him hostage, but one of Dahl's men shot the German in the head. This harrowing experience immediately dispelled whatever romantic notions Dahl might have had about the glamor of war, and he knew it from that moment on as a grisly business.

Two months after the war was declared, Dahl decided to enlist in the Royal Air Force (RAF). He obtained a leave of absence from Shell and drove 600 miles to Nairobi, where the RAF's regional headquarters was located. The military physician who examined him pronounced him fit for duty but expressed some reservations about the wisdom of cramming Dahl's six-and-a-half-foot frame into the cockpit of an airplane. Dahl spent eight weeks in Nairobi learning the basics of flying and was then transferred to a base in Iraq to complete his instruction. He trained in Iraq for six months, after which he was promoted to the rank of pilot officer. The RAF decided to use him as a fighter pilot and assigned him to the 80 Squadron, which was then fighting the Italians in the Western Desert of Libya.

Rendezvousing with his squadron proved to be a near-fatal mission for Dahl. He was supposed to fly a fighter biplane from a RAF station near the Suez Canal to the squadron's airfield in the middle of the desert. In order to fly this distance, he needed to make several stops to refuel. On the last of these stops a commanding officer gave him instructions to find the squadron's airfield, but the instructions were off by some 50 miles. When Dahl reached the spot to which he had been sent, he saw nothing but the rocky desert. He circled the area but still saw no sign of the airfield. At this point he was running out of fuel, and it was nearly too dark to fly. He had no choice, he concluded, but to attempt a landing in the desert. He put the plane down on the most level stretch of ground that he could find, but the undercarriage struck a boulder, and the plane burst into flames. Through great exertion Dahl climbed out of the cockpit and crawled away from the burning plane before losing consciousness.

Luckily for Dahl, the smoke from his burning plane attracted the attention of some British soldiers patrolling the area. They drove out to investigate and found Dahl alive but seriously hurt. They rescued him and sent him immediately to a military hospital in Alexandria, Egypt. The doctors were especially worried about Dahl's head injuries. His nose required extensive plastic surgery, and his eyes were swollen shut for weeks. He also suffered injuries to his spine and hips. It took six months before he was well enough to be discharged from the hospital. This period was a very trying one for Dahl. The pain and the loneliness ate at him, as did the meaninglessness of the whole episode. He found it difficult to accept the fact that he had nearly lost his life simply because a commanding officer had given careless instructions.

Upon his discharge from the hospital, Dahl spent several weeks convalescing in Alexandria and then reported to the RAF medical examiners in Cairo to see if he was fit to resume flying. Much to Dahl's relief, they allowed him to rejoin his old squadron, which at that point was stationed in Greece. Flying a Mark 1 Hurricane, Dahl made his way across the Mediterranean Sea and landed at an aerodrome near Athens on 14 April 1941. He quickly learned that the 80 Squadron and the other British forces in Greece were on the verge of being driven out of the country by the much larger and vastly better-equipped German forces. Dahl spent the next 10 days attacking bombers, providing ships with air cover, and engaging German fighter planes in dogfights. Although Dahl and the other pilots flew up to four missions a day, they barely slowed down the advancing Germans. Finally, after the squadron had been reduced from 15 planes to a mere five, Dahl and a few of the other surviving pilots were pulled out of Greece and flown to Egypt.

Dahl left Greece with nothing but his flight log, but what he lacked in luggage he made up for in vivid memories. In those 10 days he had been transformed from an inexperienced fighter pilot into a seasoned veteran. He had shot down several planes, survived numerous air battles, and proven that he could handle a plane in the worst possible flying conditions. All of this helped bolster his self-confidence. His experiences, though, gave him cause to question the wisdom of his superiors. As John Terraine points out in *A Time for Courage: The Royal Air Force in the European War, 1939–1945,* the RAF's campaign in Greece amounted to little more than a fiasco.[6] The poor planning and serious strategic errors that plagued the campaign were readily apparent to Dahl and the other pilots. Time and again they were sent into hopeless battles or ordered to carry out pointless missions. On one occasion, for example, they were ordered to provide air cover for the Royal Navy, but when they arrived at the area to which they had been sent, the ships were nowhere to be seen. Although these problems did not undermine Dahl's resolve to fight, he became increasingly reluctant to suspend his independent judgment.

Following the debacle in Greece, the RAF gathered together the remaining pilots of the 80 Squadron, supplied them with new Hurricanes, and sent them to Syria to fight the pro-Nazi Vichy French, who rose to power after Germany defeated France. Beginning in late May 1941, Dahl and his fellow fighter pilots resumed the hectic pace of the Grecian campaign. On one exceptionally frantic day Dahl stayed in the air for over eight hours. Four weeks into the campaign, however, he began experiencing crippling headaches during dogfights. A medical examination revealed that the head injuries he had suffered earlier were the cause of the headaches. Worried that Dahl might lose consciousness while in the air, the squadron doctor refused to allow him to fly. Dahl was sent back to England on leave as an invalid. Although he felt bitterly disappointed that his flying days were over, the prospect of seeing his family again filled him with happiness.

The trip to England took several weeks, and once he arrived he had some problems locating his family, since they had moved. He had a month's leave, most of which he spent at his mother's recently purchased cottage in the village of Grendon Underwood. When he reported back to duty the RAF was not sure how best to use his skills. Initially, they planned for him to be a flight instructor, but he needed to overcome his medical problems before he could do this job. He was therefore placed in a rehabilitation program. During this period he met Harold Balfour, the under-secretary of state for air (RAF), who decided to send Dahl to Washington, D.C., as assistant air attaché.

Dahl arrived in America in January 1942 and began working at the British Embassy. Although he was officially serving in a low-level diplomatic position, part of his job involved intelligence work. At that point the United States had just entered the war, and the British wanted to know what they could expect from the Americans. To this end Dahl got to know a number of powerful political figures, including Franklin Roosevelt, Henry Wallace, and Harry Truman. When he heard information that might affect the British war effort, he reported it to the British Secret Intelligence Service. In 1943 he was summoned back to England in order to meet with the head of the secret service. He was then promoted to the rank of wing commander and sent back to America, where he remained for the duration of the war.[7]

Dahl excelled as a spy, in part because his personality was well suited for such work. An independent spirit such as Dahl's is something of an impediment in most military jobs, but it is necessary in spy work. His job required that he work in isolation and without much direct supervision, but for Dahl this posed few problems. His outsider mentality helped him to remain somewhat detached from the people upon whom he was spying, so that his personal feelings did not interfere with his work. Finally, his inherent distrust of rules and societal conventions suited nicely when his spying necessitated the violation of a rule or two.

## Early Writing Career

Dahl began his writing career quite by accident. Shortly after he arrived at the British Embassy, Dahl met C. S. Forester, the celebrated English writer of nautical novels, including the Captain Hornblower series. At the time Forester worked for the British Information Services and was writing articles designed to heighten American interest in the war. Since Dahl was one of the few people in Washington who had seen action, Forester decided to write an article about him for the *Saturday Evening Post,* which was always ready to publish his work. Forester arranged a luncheon with Dahl in order to interview him about his most exciting experience as a pilot. During the meal, when it became clear that taking detailed notes and eating roast duck at the same time was not easy for the celebrated novelist, Dahl volunteered to jot down some notes about his crash in Libya and send them to Forester. That evening Dahl sat down at his desk, but instead of making a few notes, he wrote a full-scale article, which he entitled "A Piece of Cake." In the morning one of the secretaries at the embassy typed it up, and Dahl put it in the mail to Forester.

Forester so liked Dahl's story that he had his agent send it to the *Saturday Evening Post* completely untouched. The editors of the *Post* accepted it, but they made one significant change before publishing it. Instead of using Dahl's title, "A Piece of Cake," they called it "Shot Down over Libya," thus beginning an inaccuracy that followed Dahl for many years. In his letter conveying the news about the story's acceptance, Forester said, "Your piece is marvelous. It is the work of a gifted writer. . . . The *Post* is asking if you will write more stories for them. I do hope you will. Did you know you were a writer?" (*Wonderful,* 198–99). Dahl had never before considered writing as a possible career, but after reading Forester's letter he began to think quite seriously about it.

Dahl took to spending his evenings at home writing a series of stories on the theme of flying. Although he drew heavily on his own experiences as a fighter pilot, he made no attempt to record them in a factual manner. This experiment in writing fiction proved highly successful. Not only did he enjoy writing these stories, but he also succeeded in getting all of them published in prominent American magazines, including the *Atlantic Monthly, Harper's, Ladies' Home Journal,* and *Collier's.*

Dahl also tried his hand at writing a children's fantasy about tiny creatures called gremlins who sabotaged RAF fighter planes. Walt Disney Productions purchased the story and set out to make a film version of it. The film never materialized, but Disney did arrange for the story to be published in book form. Entitled *The Gremlins,* the book appeared in 1943 and included numerous color illustrations by Disney himself (*Wonderful,* 200–201).

When World War II came to a close in 1945, Dahl faced a turning point in his life. With his military career over, he had to decide whether he should go back to Shell Oil or become a full-time writer. There was no question in his mind as to what he should do. He had now sold about 16 short stories to major American magazines and had never had a rejection. Moreover, the independent life-style that went with being a writer appealed to him immensely. He informed Shell of his decision not to return, and they gave him his provident fund, which amounted to about £1,000. He moved back to England to share a house with his mother and his one remaining unmarried sister in the small town of Amersham in Buckinghamshire.[8]

One of the first steps Dahl took in his effort to support himself through his writing was to collect 10 of his flying stories into a book called *Over to You.* The now-defunct publishing firm of Reynal and Hitchcock in New York brought out the book in late 1945.

It attracted the attention of the famous editor Maxwell Perkins, who contacted Dahl and asked him to write a novel. Although Dahl felt much more comfortable writing short stories, he was intrigued by Perkins's request and agreed to work on the novel. Using some of the ideas he had originally articulated in *The Gremlins,* he wrote an apocalyptic fantasy novel about gremlins, world wars, and human fallibility. He hoped that once he finished the first draft, Perkins would help him revise it. Unfortunately, Perkins died shortly after Dahl sent him the manuscript, and Perkins's successor went ahead and published the novel without any revisions. Entitled *Some Time Never: A Fable for Supermen,* the book was published by Scribner's in 1948 and met with a mixed response from the critics. Dahl viewed the book as a failure and decided to return to writing short stories (West 1990, 62–63).

During the late 1940s and early 1950s Dahl quietly established himself as a leading short-story writer. Every year he produced two or three stories, all of which appeared in the *New Yorker, Harper's,* and other prestigious American periodicals. Generally macabre in nature, his stories won praise for their vivid details, carefully constructed plots, and surprise endings. He did most of his writing in a quiet country cottage owned by his mother. When not working he pursued several hobbies, including breeding and racing greyhounds, gardening, and collecting paintings, wines, and antiques.[9] In addition to helping him relax, his hobbies often provided him with material for his stories.

Every year he took a trip to New York City to confer with editors and to visit friends. One of his closest American friends, a newspaper publisher named Charles Marsh, urged Dahl to spend more time in New York. Marsh argued that it would be good for Dahl's career to be in closer contact with the New York literary establishment. Dahl agreed and gradually prolonged his visits, eventually finding it necessary to rent a small apartment in the city (Farrell, 71).

In 1952 Dahl was in New York looking for a publisher for *Someone Like You,* his second short-story collection. He was mulling over offers from several publishers when the telephone in his apartment rang. Dahl answered it, and a voice said, "This is

Alfred Knopf." Dahl was astounded to be speaking to such a famous publisher. "Look," Knopf said, "I've just read your short story "Taste" in the *New Yorker*. Do you have any more?" Dahl informed him that he was just finishing a book of stories, and Knopf said, "I'll buy it" (West 1990, 63). Dahl readily accepted the offer, and Knopf published the book in 1953.

While arranging for the publication of *Someone Like You* Dahl received an invitation to a dinner party hosted by Lillian Hellman. At the time Hellman was staging a revival of her play *The Children's Hour,* and a number of the dinner guests were involved in the production. One of the leading actresses in the play, Patricia Neal, was seated next to Dahl, and though Dahl paid little attention to her at the time, there was something about this famous actress from Tennessee that attracted him. The next night he asked her out, but she turned him down. He persisted, and she finally agreed to see him.[10] After an eight-month courtship Dahl and Neal married on 2 July 1953.

They took an apartment in New York and stayed there during the winter months, but they spent their summers in England. In 1954 they purchased an old farmhouse in Great Missenden, a village located about 30 miles west of London, and this became something of a home base for them. Dahl especially liked this house, for it was near his mother and two of his sisters, and it had a lot of space for gardens. In the apple orchard that came with the house, Dahl built, for only £100, a small brick hut in which to write. For the rest of his life this tiny, cold hut, cluttered with manuscripts, galleys, and files, was where Dahl went to write.[11]

The first seven or so years of Dahl's married life went rather smoothly. He and Neal worked out a schedule that allowed them both to pursue their careers as well as to care for their growing family. With the births of Olivia in 1954, Tessa in 1957, and Theo in 1960, Dahl had a full dose of parenthood. For Dahl the family had always been a source of meaning and comfort, and now that he had children of his own, he threw himself into the role of caring father. He spent many hours playing with the children, telling them stories, and watching them grow, but he never stopped writing. He always wrote strictly on schedule: 10 A.M. to noon and 4 P.M. to 6 P.M., seven days a week.

Early in 1955 he wrote a play called *The Honeys*. Based on some of the stories from *Someone Like You,* the play revolves around two sisters who decide to murder their husbands. *The Honeys* opened on Broadway on 28 April 1955 and starred Hume Cronyn, Jessica Tandy, and Dorothy Stickney. Although it received some good notices, it ran for only 36 performances. Its short run, combined with the difficulties that Dahl had with the play's director, convinced Dahl to stick to short-story writing.

He continued to publish macabre short stories in the *New Yorker* and other American magazines until he had enough for a third collection. Published in early 1960 under the title *Kiss Kiss,* this collection of 11 stories received many rave reviews, but a few critics felt that he was beginning to repeat himself. Writing for the *Saturday Review,* Granville Hicks, for example, said that the "trickiness" of Dahl's plots could easily "degenerate into mere formula, and, though this has not happened with Dahl, there are one or two stories that seem slightly mechanical."[12] While Dahl had no fear that he would become a formula writer, he knew that continually coming up with new plots was not an easy task. There were days when he could not think of a new plot, and it was on one of those days that he decided to "have a go at doing a children's book" (West 1990, 63).

## Later Writing Career

Dahl's decision to write for children was a direct outgrowth of his parenting experiences. He had already been making up bedtime stories for Olivia and Tessa, and some of these stories were very popular with the girls. They especially seemed to like a story about a peach that went on growing until it became a gigantic fruit, and Dahl decided to take this story and expand it into a children's book. As he recalled a few years later, the book "took somewhere between eight or nine months to complete, with no time off for other work, and eight or nine months is a big slice out of the life of any writer, and a big drain on his batteries."[13] He entitled the completed manuscript *James and the Giant Peach* and sold it to Knopf, who published it in 1961.

Even before *James and the Giant Peach* was published, Dahl began writing another children's book, which he tentatively entitled *Charlie's Chocolate Boy* (Nichols, 8). Family crises, however, forced him to put it aside for several years. The first of these crises involved Dahl's son, Theo. On 5 December 1960 the children's nanny took Theo, who was then four months old, out for a stroll in his baby carriage. She was crossing a busy New York City street when a taxi hit the carriage. Theo suffered head injuries that led to the accumulation of fluid on his brain. To remove this fluid, his doctors implanted a shunt. Unfortunately, the shunt often became blocked and needed to be replaced, resulting in numerous operations (Farrell, 152–54).

Determined to do something to help Theo, Dahl set to work on designing an improved shunt. He contacted Stanley Wade, a mechanical engineer, and Kenneth Till, a neurosurgeon, and the three of them developed a new shunt that became known as the Dahl-Wade-Till Valve. Although Theo no longer needed it by the time it was perfected, the shunt went into use around the world (Farrell, 15–17).

After Theo's brush with death, Dahl and Neal decided to make Great Missenden their permanent home. New York, they felt, posed too many dangers for young children. They enrolled Olivia and Tessa in a school located a short way from their home, and every afternoon one of them would drive to the school and pick up the girls. One afternoon in the autumn of 1962 Olivia came home with a note saying that she had been exposed to measles. There was no immunization against measles available in England at the time. Olivia soon contracted the disease, but instead of recovering quickly, as the family doctor had predicted, she developed a rare complication called measles encephalitis. On 17 November 1962 she died (Farrell, 134–35).

Olivia's death put a tremendous strain on Dahl. In his despair he found it very difficult to concentrate on his writing. He remained in a writing slump for about a year and a half, but he began to revive when he learned that Neal was expecting another child. With the birth of Ophelia on 12 May 1964, Dahl felt ready to return to his writing in earnest.

Now that he felt capable of writing again, Dahl went back to the children's book he had begun in 1961. Dissatisfied with the early drafts of the story, he completely revised it and changed its title to *Charlie and the Chocolate Factory.* Knopf published the book in late 1964, and it soon became a best-seller. Around that time the publishing firm of Crowell-Collier asked him to contribute a children's story to an anthology that they planned to produce. The idea behind the anthology was to have some of the leading writers for adults each contribute a children's story. Dahl sent in a story about a girl with a magic finger. Although the editors liked Dahl's story, they were disappointed with the other contributions and decided against publishing the anthology. Thus the story went unpublished until 1966, when it came out as a picture book entitled *The Magic Finger* (Powling, 67).

As 1964 came to a close, Dahl and the rest of the family felt that their troubles were finally behind them. Dahl and Neal were working, the children were healthy, and a new baby was on the way. Earlier Neal had agreed to spend the first few months of 1965 in Los Angeles working on a film, and it was decided that the whole family would accompany her. For their first several weeks in Los Angeles all went well, but then another crisis shook the family. On 17 February 1965 Neal suffered a massive stroke. The doctors at the Medical Center of the University of California at Los Angeles saved her life, but she lost much of her physical and mental abilities. During the next year or so Dahl concerned himself primarily with caring for the children and helping Neal recover. She gradually regained her speech and coordination, and in August she gave birth to a healthy girl, whom they named Lucy. Neal's stroke and subsequent recovery attracted much media attention and was even the subject of a book by Barry Farrell called *Pat and Roald.*

In addition to causing a great deal of stress in the family, Neal's stroke created financial problems. The couple's bills kept mounting, and Neal was in no position to help pay them. When movie producer Albert Broccoli offered Dahl an opportunity to write the screenplay for the James Bond movie *You Only Live Twice,* he jumped at it, for he knew that successful screenwriters often had tremendous incomes. Dahl wrote the screenplay during the winter of 1965, and the film was shot in the summer of 1966. Dahl had not pursued this form of writing in the past because he disliked having to work with directors and producers, but he got along well with everyone associated with the Bond movie (Farrell, 152–54). His positive experiences with that movie led him to write screenplays for two more: *Chitty Chitty Bang Bang* in 1967 and *Willy Wonka and the Chocolate Factory* in 1970. The directors of those movies, however, made so many changes in Dahl's screenplays that he vowed never to write another (Powling, 55–64).

During the early 1970s Dahl's life stabilized. With Neal well enough to work again and their children all old enough to attend school, Dahl found it easier to concentrate on his writing. Over the course of the decade, Dahl published five books for children. The first, *Fantastic Mr. Fox,* came out in 1970, followed by *Charlie and the Great Glass Elevator* in 1972. In 1975 Dahl revised one of his short stories for adults into a children's book called *Danny, the Champion of the World.* His next children's book, an anthology entitled *The Wonderful Story of Henry Sugar and Six Others,* appeared in 1977. Consisting of three essays and four stories, this book marked Dahl's first attempt to tap into the young-adult market. A year later he published *The Enormous Crocodile,* a picture book illustrated by Quentin Blake. This was but the first of many books on which Dahl and Blake collaborated.

Dahl's literary creations of the 1970s also included some works for adult readers. He wrote several lengthy stories dealing with sexuality, most of which appeared in *Playboy.* In 1974 Knopf published a collection of four of these stories under the title *Switch Bitch.* The main character in two of these stories, a promiscuous world traveler named Oswald Hendryks Cornelius, so appealed to Dahl that he went on to write an entire novel about the character's exploits. Entitled *My Uncle Oswald,* the novel appeared in 1979. It was Dahl's first novel since *Some Time Never,* and like its predecessor, it met with mixed reviews, but it has remained in print and is much read today.

Although he remained productive throughout the 1970s, Dahl's life was not without its complications. His health deteriorated, and problems with his spine and hips caused him considerable pain. He underwent a series of operations to correct these problems, but the pain never completely disappeared. His marriage also deteriorated during this period. After several strained years he and Neal separated in 1979. He remained in Great Missenden, and she moved to New York. Four years later they were divorced, and soon thereafter Dahl married Felicity Crosland.

Dahl began calling himself an old man in the 1980s, but unlike many old men, he did not slow down. If anything, he began to work harder. From 1980 until his death on 23 November 1990, he wrote well over a book per year. Although he wrote mostly for children, he did not write the same type of book over and over again. He published three full-scale fantasies for intermediate readers: *The BFG* (1982), *The Witches* (1983), and *Matilda* (1988). For beginning readers he wrote *The Twits* (1980), *George's Marvelous Medicine* (1981), *The Giraffe and the Pelly and Me* (1985), *Esio Trot* (1990), and *The Minpins* (1991). He also wrote a rather risqué short story for adults and older children, which was posthumously published in book form under the title *The Vicar of Nibbleswicke* (1991). During this same period he wrote three books of verse: *Revolting Rhymes* (1982), *Dirty Beasts* (1983), and *Rhyme Stew* (1989). The decade also saw the publication of his first books of nonfiction. In 1984 he published *Boy: Tales of Childhood*, an autobiographical work, which was followed by *Going Solo* (1986), a book about his years in Africa and the Royal Air Force. Dahl wrote *Boy* for children, but he directed *Going Solo* at more mature readers.

In the 1980s Dahl's books for children began to receive praise from critics and scholars. Before this time his books had been extremely popular among children but were often condemned by adult critics who found them vulgar, excessively violent, and disrespectful toward adults. Starting around 1981, however, a number of critics refuted these charges. Alasdair Campbell began this trend with an article published in the *School Librarian*. He analyzed the children's books that Dahl had published up to that point and concluded that all but *Charlie and the Great Glass Elevator* were of high literary quality.[14] Over the next several years

Charles Sarland, Hamida Bosmajian, and other critics also published scholarly defenses of Dahl's children's books. At the same time his children's books began winning awards, including the prestigious Whitbread Award for *The Witches*. In announcing this award the Whitbread judges said, "From the first paragraph to the last, we felt we were in the hands of a master." Thus, at the time of his death, Dahl had achieved in children's literature what he had achieved in adult literature in the 1950s—immense popularity as well as critical acclaim.

# 2

# Flying into Writing

During the beginning stages of Dahl's career as an author, he experimented with several different writing forms, including nonfiction, short stories, a screenplay, and a novel. No matter what form his writing took, however, he always drew on his experiences as a pilot in the Royal Air Force. He did not, though, write partriotic war stories with dashing heroes and cunning enemies. Dahl was interested in the interior lives of the RAF pilots. He wrote mostly about their fears and fantasies, their responses to danger, and their attempts to form relationships. He probed their emotional states both while they were flying and while they were on the ground. In some cases he wrote from personal experience, but often he relied on his observations of other pilots.

## "A Piece of Cake"

Dahl's first publication, an autobiographical essay about the time his plane crashed in Libya, was published anonymously in the 1 August 1942 issue of the *Saturday Evening Post*. As previously noted, Dahl intended the essay to be entitled "A Piece of Cake," but the editors used the more dramatic (but inaccurate) title "Shot Down over Libya." When the essay was anthologized, however, Dahl took the opportunity to restore the original title as well as to make a number of other changes.

Before writing this essay Dahl had written only letters and school papers and had little confidence in his writing ability. He was therefore quite surprised at how easily the words came. Decades later Dahl still remembered how he felt while he wrote this essay: "I started at seven o'clock and finished at midnight. I remember I had a glass of Portuguese brandy to keep me going. For the first time in my life, I became totally absorbed in what I was doing. . . . It was astonishing how everything came back to me with absolute clarity. Writing it down on paper was not difficult. The story seemed to be telling itself, and the hand that held the pencil moved rapidly back and forth across each page" (*Wonderful,* 198).

Although ostensibly about the crash of Dahl's fighter plane in the Western Desert of Libya, the essay provides little information about the actual crash. The events preceding the crash, as well as its cause, are left indefinite. Dahl simply says that "there was trouble, lots and lots of trouble."[1] The core of the essay focuses on the events that happened immediately after the plane hit the ground. Unlike the introductory section, this part of the essay is replete with details. Dahl describes his thought processes as he tried to climb out of the plane, his shock at discovering that his nose was gone, and his dreams while lying unconscious in the hospital.

Running throughout the essay is a grim sense of humor. This quality is especially evident in the pages that deal with Dahl's struggle to get out of the plane. As he describes it, his brain and his body lost their synchronization. The brain knew how to get out of the plane but not how much damage the body had sustained. The body sensed injuries and restraints but could do nothing about them. In the essay Dahl's brain and body communicate through a slow telegraph system. For example, the body sends the following message to the brain when the plane catches on fire:

"Down here there is a great hotness. What shall we do? (Signed) Left Leg and Right Leg" (*Over,* 44). Initially, this playful approach to describing a near-fatal accident adds a touch of levity; eventually, it helps create a sense of panic, for the reader realizes that Dahl's chances of survival diminished with every additional second he stayed in the plane.

In the second half of the essay Dahl provides a vivid account of the dreams he had during the four days he was unconscious in a hospital in Alexandria, Egypt. In one of the dreams Dahl and his fellow pilots attempt to foil the enemy by painting jokes and humorous pictures on the RAF planes. The idea, as one of the people in the dream explains, is that the "German pilots will . . . shake so with their laughing that they won't be able to shoot straight" (*Over,* 44). While he is still dreaming Dahl realizes that the idea will not work because the jokes are written in English, and nobody knows how to translate them into German. Another dream begins with Dahl being shot down while he is flying his plane and ends with Dahl trying to convince a nurse that he is still alive. The final dream is filled with images associated with death. In this dream he runs through a field and suddenly falls off a cliff. He grabs at branches as he falls but to no avail; nothing can stop his plunge into darkness.

Even though "A Piece of Cake" is a work of nonfiction, it anticipates the fiction that Dahl went on to write. Grim humor and dream imagery, both of which he uses in this essay, often figure in his short stories. The essay also marks the first appearance of a major theme in Dahl's writing: the human response to impending death. On a more abstract level the essay records an event that in Dahl's opinion helped transform him into a writer. According to Dahl, he had the mind-set of a businessman before the crash, but afterwards he began thinking more like a writer. The brush with death and the time he spent convalescing in the hospital made him more introspective and creative. He began paying attention to his dreams and fantasies and developed an interest in aesthetics.[2] Thus, the events described in "A Piece of Cake" can be seen as important bricks in the foundation of Dahl's literary career.

## *The Gremlins*

Dahl began writing fiction shortly after he finished "A Piece of Cake." He chose as the subject for his first story a race of tiny mythological creatures called gremlins. Though sometimes credited with inventing the name for these creatures, Dahl never claimed to have done so. "I didn't invent the word," he said during an interview. "It was being knocked about in my squadron and maybe other squadrons, too" (West 1990, 62). In the story he embellished on the folklore about gremlins and worked in a little autobiographical material, producing a whimsical and somewhat nostalgic picture of life in the Royal Air Force.

Set in England during the famous Battle of Britain, the story begins with Gus, a RAF fighter pilot, discovering that his plane is being sabotaged by a drill-wielding gremlin. The gremlin wears suction boots that enable him to stand on the moving plane to bore holes in its wings and engine. Gus succeeds in landing the disabled plane, but he is less successful in convincing the other pilots to believe in gremlins. Soon, though, the gremlins make themselves visible to the entire squadron. They explain that they became airplane saboteurs after the RAF built a factory in the middle of the woods where the gremlins had lived for centuries.

Not long after meeting the gremlins, Gus is wounded as a result of a plane crash. During his stay in the hospital Gus figures out a way to train the gremlins to become more friendly toward the RAF pilots. His plan works, and he eventually becomes quite close to the gremlins. These newfound friends come to Gus's aid when the doctors rule that he is not longer fit to fly. The gremlins tell Gus to request another examination, and this time the gremlins make sure that Gus passes. As the story ends Gus is "able to return to his flying."[3] Thus, in some ways, the plot parallels Dahl's own experience of being injured in a crash and prohibited from flying because of the injuries. The major difference, of course, is that Dahl never passed the examination.

The story's whimsical quality is enhanced by the details that

Dahl provides about the gremlins. Dahl describes the typical male gremlin as "scarcely more than six inches high, with a large round face and a little pair of horns growing out of his head" (*Gremlins*). Female gremlins, called fifinellas, look similar to the males but have curly horns. The name Dahl uses for young gremlins is widgets. He explains that "no one knows until they grow up whether they are going to turn into males or females, but it's usually males; in each nest of twelve widgets only one will eventually turn into a fifinella" (*Gremlins*). According to Dahl, most gremlins live underground, but a special breed of gremlins, known as spandules, live in cumulus clouds. Although Dahl gives gremlins many strange qualities, perhaps their most peculiar attribute is their fondness for eating used postage stamps.

Upon finishing the story Dahl showed it to Sidney Bernstein of the British Information Services, and Bernstein sent it to Walt Disney. The manuscript arrived on 1 July 1942, and Disney immediately decided to buy the story and turn it into a film. Soon thereafter Disney flew Dahl to Hollywood for three weeks to help write the screenplay. Production work began in October, and the first test reels were done in November. In an effort to generate interest in the film, Disney arranged to have the story published in *Cosmopolitan* in December 1942, but Dahl did not attach his name to the story at that time; instead, he used the pseudonym Pegasus. About six months later Random House published a somewhat revised version of the story as a picture book entitled *The Gremlins*. This time the author was listed as Flight Lieutenant Roald Dahl. Soon after the publication of the book, Disney lost interest in the project, and work on the film came to a halt in September 1943.[4]

Although disappointed that the film had been abandoned, Dahl took satisfaction in the positive reactions to the book. Eleanor Roosevelt, for example, read the book to her grandchildren and liked it so much that she invited Dahl to have dinner with her and President Roosevelt (*Wonderful,* 201–2). The book also received several favorable reviews, including a highly complimentary notice in the *New York Times Book Review*. The author of this review,

E. L. Buell, praised Dahl for his "adeptness in building up a tall tale in the American tradition."[5] Encouraged by these responses, Dahl began writing fiction on a regular basis.

## Over to You

In the mid-1940s Dahl wrote a number of stories about the experiences of pilots during the war, most of which appeared in *Atlantic Monthly, Ladies' Home Journal, Harper's,* and other American magazines. Shortly after the war ended he collected "A Piece of Cake," six of his magazine stories, and three previously unpublished stories and arranged to have them published as an anthology. Reynal and Hitchcock, a small New York publisher, released the collection in late 1945 under the title of *Over to You: Ten Stories of Flyers and Flying.*

The stories in *Over to You* vary in several significant ways. Some are realistic, some border on the surreal, and some are outright works of fantasy. Some have fully developed plots, while others are vignettes. Several take place during the heat of battle, but others are set away from the fighting. Although most are serious, some have touches of humor, and one is uproariously funny. Despite their differences, however, almost all of these stories feature characters who struggle against the dehumanizing aspects of war. Dahl's characters, though surrounded by killing, often attempt to preserve life, right wrongs, and reach out to others.

Perhaps the most realistic story in the collection is "Katina." Originally published in *Ladies' Home Journal* in March 1944, this is one of the first stories that Dahl wrote after the publication of *The Gremlins.* "Katina" is a direct outgrowth of the experiences that Dahl had while fighting in Greece. The story is set in the places where Dahl stayed during his brief time in Greece, and many of the events that are mentioned in the story actually happened to him. Although the story includes a character who is modeled after Dahl, this character is more of an observer. The central character is Katina, a Greek girl whose family is killed when the Germans bomb their town. Some RAF pilots discover her after the bombing and take her to their sick bay to have her wounds dressed. Since she has no place else to go, she is adopted by the squadron. The pilots feed her, buy her new clothing, and try to teach her English. They even add her name to the squadron's official records. Katina provides the pilots with a sense of purpose. In a way she is their connection to the Greek people whom they are trying to defend, but she is more than that; she also serves as their connection to humanity. Although these pilots are faced with the likelihood of death and the certainty of defeat, they forget their isolation and hopelessness when they are caring for Katina.

Another story in which pilots function as rescuers is "Madame Rosette." In this story two of the pilots involved in fighting the Italians in Libya are granted a 48-hour pass, which they spend in Cairo. Stuffy, the younger of the two, is attracted to a young woman whom he sees in a store. He tells Stag, his companion, about the woman, and Stag says that it could be arranged for Stuffy to spend the night with her. All Stuffy needs to do is call Madame Rosette, the owner of Cairo's largest brothel, and she will coerce the young woman into sleeping with him. It will cost a great deal, but Stuffy has enough money to pay the fee. Stuffy makes the call, but then he begins to have misgivings about the transaction. After talking with Stag about the way Madame Rosette treats her employees, he realizes that the woman to whom he is attracted will be seriously hurt if he goes through with his plan. Not only does he decide to call off the deal, but he and Stag embark on a mission to free all the prostitutes in Madame Rosette's brothel.

Humor plays a major role in "Madame Rosette," but it is not the whimsical sort of humor that runs through *The Gremlins*. The humor in "Madame Rosette" is closely tied to more serious emotions. Like the pilots in "Katina," Stuffy and Stag have seen so much "action" that they are in danger of becoming immune to human suffering. Their war experiences have conditioned them not to think immediately about how their actions might affect other people. For Stuffy and Stag, however, this apparent callousness is not deep-seated. As they demonstrate in rescuing the prostitutes, they are still capable of feeling compassion and empathy and acting on these feelings. Thus, the story is not just a frolicsome tale about pilots and prostitutes; it is also a celebration of the compassionate side of human nature.

The three fantasy stories in the collection also feature characters who, in the midst of war, try to make meaningful connections with other people. These stories, entitled "Death of an Old Old Man," "They Shall Never Grow Old," and "Only This," all begin realistically but soon move beyond reality. In all three cases the fantasy elements come into play when the central characters confront death. These characters transcend the horror and loneliness of death by reaching out to others.

"Death of an Old Old Man," the lead story in the book, deals with a pilot whose plane becomes disabled during a dogfight over Holland. His adversary, a German pilot, suffers the same fate, and the two of them bail out and parachute to the ground, where they continue their battle. While they are engaged in hand-to-hand combat, the English pilot suddenly stops struggling. He forgets about the man who is trying to kill him and begins to imagine a better future, a future in which he will no longer be alone. "There is a girl somewhere that I wish to sleep with," he thinks, "and you cannot sleep struggling with a girl. You cannot do anything struggling; especially you cannot live struggling, and so now I'm going to do all the things that I want to do, and there will be no more struggling" (*Over,* 22). He then leaves his body and for the first time in years feels happy and relaxed.

The central character in "They Shall Not Grow Old" is a young pilot named Fin. At the beginning of the story Fin volunteers to fly a reconnaissance mission. Since he only needs to fly a short distance, his fellow pilots expect the mission to take no more than two hours. When he does not return after about three hours, the other pilots assume that he has crashed. The next day, however, Fin returns, but he has no memory of what had happened to him while he was missing. Finally, after witnessing another pilot crash, Fin recalls what had occurred during his disappearance. As he tells the other pilots, he had flown into a thick cloud, and some unknown force had taken control of his plane. He had soon found himself flying in formation with hundreds of other planes, whose pilots "were all waving at each other" (*Over,* 125). The planes had headed toward a beautiful landing field, but when it had been Fin's turn to land, his plane would not touch down. Although he had desperately wanted to land and to be with the other pilots, his plane had climbed back into the air and returned to the cloud in which his strange odyssey had begun. The pilots to whom Fin tells his story believe him, but they still react with surprise when they discover that Fin no longer fears death.

"They Shall Not Grow Old" has several direct parallels to the story of Valhalla from Norse mythology. As Dahl must have known, given his familiarity with Norse mythology, Valhalla is a massive hall in which slain warriors spend eternity enjoying feasts, sports, and each other's company. The warriors are chosen by a group of maidens known as the Valkyries. In the earliest versions of the myth the Valkyries are associated with clouds. Thus, the place that Fin is taken can be seen as a sort of Valhalla for pilots, and the cloud that seems to take control of his plane can be seen as a Valkyrie. The most significant parallel, however, is that in both stories a special camaraderie exists among the fighters, even after they have died.

"Only This" also involves a special relationship, but in this case it is between a bomber pilot and his mother. One night she wakes up with a premonition that her son is in danger. As she sits in her chair, worrying about his safety, she has a sense of being in the cockpit with him. At the same time, the pilot senses his mother's presence, but he can do little more than give her a smile before his plane is hit. The mother watches while he tries to steady the plane long enough for the crew to bail out, and then she sees him collapse. Her reaction to this vision makes for a surprising but poignant conclusion to the story. Even though "Only This" is one of the saddest stories in the collection, the unusual nature of the characters' relationship offers some comfort. They are not able to avoid tragedy, but at least they do not have to face it entirely alone.

Of the remaining stories, "Someone Like You" and "An African Story" are especially noteworthy, for they feature characters who differ significantly from the others in the collection. The characters in most of the stories in *Over to You* are generally heroic. They may have some flaws, but they almost always act bravely and with compassion. The characters in "Someone Like You" and "An African Story," however, do not fit this mold.

"Someone Like You" takes place in a pub shortly before the war's end. As the story opens, two pilots who have not seen each other for five years get together to talk and drink. One of the men is a bomber pilot, and he begins talking about jinking. He says that every time he went on a bombing raid, he thought, "Shall I just jink a little; shall I swerve a fraction to one side, then my bombs will fall on someone else. I keep thinking, whom shall I make them fall on; whom shall I kill tonight" (*Over,* 152). Later in their conversation the bomber pilot gestures at the crowd in the pub and asks, "Wouldn't there be a bloody row if they were all suddenly dead; if they all suddenly fell off their chairs on to the floor dead?" (*Over,* 157). After the other pilot agrees that there would be a row, the bomber pilot says, "Well. I've done that. . . . I've killed more people than there are in this room hundreds of times. So have you" (*Over,* 157–58). At this point the men become uncomfortable in the pub, but they want to keep drinking. The story closes with the men seeking another pub—either one with no people in it or one filled with thousands of people.

The bomber pilot in "Someone Like You" is the only character in the book who questions the underlying morality of carrying out bombing and strafing missions. He feels that he is somehow responsible for the deaths of many civilians, and this makes him feel immensely guilty. Other characters in Dahl's stories have difficulty accepting death, but this character has equal difficulty accepting his status as a killer. The fact that he is considered a hero by his countrymen does nothing to alleviate his feelings of guilt. For him, drinking lots of whiskey and withdrawing from society seem to be the only effective ways of dealing with the moral dilemmas that plague him.

Moral conflicts also come into play in "An African Story." On the surface, at least, this story does not deal as much with the lives of pilots as do the other stories. Although a pilot does figure in the story's introduction, the core of the story deals with an old farmer who lives in a mountainous region of Kenya. The farmer has a hired hand who helps take care of the farmer's sweet potato crop, chickens, and dairy cow. The hired hand has a sadistic personality, and one day he breaks the back of the farmer's dog because he does not like the sound that the dog makes when it licks its paws. The farmer is outraged at this act of violence but is not sure how to respond. Several days after the incident, however, the farmer thinks of a highly unusual way to get even. His plan involves the cow and a poisonous snake called a mamba. He executes his plan perfectly, but in the process he becomes as sadistic as the man he detests.

Although the old farmer in "An African Story" is not directly involved in the war, he faces a conflict that is much like the one that confronts the bomber pilot in "Someone Like You." In both cases the characters perform morally questionable acts in the process of fighting an immoral adversary. The peaceful farmer would not normally plan a murder, but when he is consumed with a desire for revenge, he finds it easy to arrange for another person's death. Similarly, the pilot would not normally massacre hundreds of civilians, but when he is ordered to drop bombs on civilian targets, he obeys. These stories, in other words, suggest that ordinary and generally decent people are capable of violence and cruelty in certain circumstances. Unlike most of the other stories, which emphasize the more noble sides of the characters' personalities, "Someone Like You" and "An African Story" explore some of the darker aspects of human nature.

Most of the reviews of *Over to You* were positive, and several reviewers predicted that Dahl would become a major figure on the literary scene. Writing for the *New York Times Book Review,* Nona Balakian commented on Dahl's "truthful" depictions of the pilots' "inner experiences" and praised his "acute awareness of the narrow margin separating shadow and substance."[6] The *Yale Review*'s Orville Prescott called the stories in *Over to You* "simple, lucid, and unpretentious" and said that Dahl was "wonderfully adept in capturing atmosphere, often in beautiful prose."[7] In a full-page article in *Saturday Review,* Michael Straight complimented Dahl's "vivid imagination" and ability to create "startling images." Straight criticized some of the stories for coming "perilously close to exchanging content for dramatic effect," but he concluded the review with a highly positive proclamation. "Dahl," he wrote, "is an author of great promise and he has written a fine and memorable book."[8]

Despite the positive reviews, *Over to You* failed to attract a large readership—partially because the publisher lacked the resources to launch an extensive promotion campaign. Also, with the war finally over, American readers were beginning to tire of war stories. The book's mediocre sales figures, however, should not obscure the fact that Dahl was already writing polished prose.

## *Some Time Never*

The critical success of *Over to You* attracted the attention of Maxwell Perkins, the celebrated editor who worked for Scribner's. Usually, the authors in whom Perkins took an interest greatly benefited from his attention, but Dahl proved to be an exception. At Perkins's encouragement Dahl wrote a novel entitled *Some Time Never: A Fable for Supermen,* which came out in 1948. As Dahl later recounted in an interview, the experience of writing the novel began on a high note, but it ended up being the low point in his literary career:

> My short stories had come to Perkins's attention, and he sent me a note that said, "Dear Mr. Dahl, would you come and see me." Well, I jumped high in the air, as any writer would in those days. He was, after all, editing Wolfe and Hemingway and Fitzgerald. He was the greatest editor America ever had. So I thought, oh wonderful, and I rushed to see him. He told me this delightful story about editing Wolfe's *Look Homeward, Angel,* and all of this was enthralling to a young writer. He then said, "These short stories of yours are lovely, but what interests me is a novel." To which I said, "But, Mr. Perkins, I don't think I can do a novel. I'm a short story writer." But he told me to go ahead and promised to help me. Well, I didn't know what to write about in a book of that length, so I expanded my gremlin story. It ended up being a rather silly

fantasy about the end of the world. It was sort of pro-
phetic, in a way, but it wasn't a good story. Well, I sent
the first draft to Perkins, but he died before he had a
chance to read it, or maybe it was my story that killed
him. The book then fell into the hands of his assistant,
who just published it as it was. (West 1990, 62–63)

The beginning of *Some Time Never* closely parallels the first
half of *The Gremlins,* but the plot is more fully developed, and the
gremlins are more sinister. Just as they had done in the earlier
story, the gremlins in *Some Time Never* wage a sort of guerrilla
war on the Royal Air Force during the early days of World War II.
For these gremlins, attacking the RAF is part of a large-scale campaign to rid the world of humans. The gremlins, who have been
living underground since the advent of the human race, plan to
move back to the Earth's surface once the humans are gone. The
book's early chapters focus on the encounters between the gremlins and an RAF pilot named Peternip. This pilot is one of the first
humans to see the gremlins and the only one to visit their underground empire. Unlike the pilot in *The Gremlins,* however, Peternip never becomes friends with the gremlins, and he does not
even try to change their behavior.

About halfway through the book, the leader of the gremlins calls
off their assault on the RAF. As he explains to the other gremlins,
he has become convinced that the human race will destroy itself
without the help of gremlins or anybody else. From this point on,
the book becomes more of a political parable than a novel. Peternip and the other human characters from the first half of the
book all but disappear. The only major character who is left is the
leader of the gremlins, and he functions as more of a commentator
than a character. He gives a series of speeches in which he details
the flaws of the human race and predicts its ultimate demise.
Although he makes many charges, he states the core of his argument toward the beginning of his first major speech:

The human creature . . . is a miserable and ill-fated giant, a mountain of conceit and selfishness, a creature

doomed now to perish at his own hands!... You know
him. You have seen him many times; a crafty and too
ingenious creature whose craft and cunning are out-
weighted only by his foolishness; a brainy creature whose
brain is great enough only to plot his own destruction,
but not so great that it can save him from himself. He is
a creature who possesses, more than any other living
creature, wisdom, but more than any other creature also
he possesses greed and avarice and a love of power.[9]

The head gremlin assures his followers that within a few decades the humans will destroy each other and leave the Earth to
the gremlins. Until then, he advises his fellow gremlins simply to
wait and enjoy the humans' final performance. As the book progresses, this prophesy comes true. Not long after World War II
ends, World War III breaks out. Unlike the other world wars, this
one does not last long, but it takes a much higher human toll. Still,
the human race does not completely disappear. The survivors soon
divide into three major power blocs: one headed by America, another led by Russia, and the third controlled by India and China.
These three blocs continue to develop new nuclear and bacterial
weapons, which they do not hesitate to use when World War IV
begins. This war finally destroys the human race, leaving the surface of the world to the patient gremlins. They soon find, however,
that it was hardly worth the wait, for the world is no longer hos-
pitable to complex life forms.

From a literary standpoint *Some Time Never* is not a successful
novel. The characters are not fully developed, the plot is dis-
jointed, and the strident writing style is reminiscent of a political
manifesto. The book's flaws did not escape the few people who
reviewed it. A reporter for *Kirkus Reviews* liked the book's satirical qualities but argued that it was not as well written as the
stories in *Over to You*.[10] The *New York Times's* reviewer thought
that the book made important points, "but they could have been
said with less repetition, less preliminary build-up and fewer
words."[11] One of the most thoughtful and sympathetic reviews appeared in *Saturday Review*. Its author, Bergen Evens, praised the

nonfantasy elements of the book and complimented Dahl for tackling the problem of self-destructive behavior, but even Evens had problems with the plot. He did not like the "cumbrousness" of the book's "supernatural machinery," and he felt that Dahl's portrayal of the gremlins was "forced" and not "in any way convincing."[12]

*Some Time Never* was quickly forgotten. Even Dahl came to see it as an apprentice piece, and he soon took to leaving it off his list of publications. The book, however, does shed light on an important change in Dahl's thoughts on human nature. In his earlier stories he generally wrote about the more noble aspects of human nature, but in this book he emphasized the flaws. The lives led by the people in *Some Time Never* recall philosopher Thomas Hobbes's pessimistic description of "the life of man [as] solitary, poor, nasty, brutish, and short."[13] Dahl's growing cynicism about human nature was related to the development and use of nuclear weapons, which he viewed as self-destructive behavior: "When man will invent and use a weapon which will purposely destroy one hundred thousand people in five seconds, when he will proceed diligently to find a means of making this weapon still more lethal, then the time has come when only man's intense conceit blinding his powers of deduction can prevent him from being quite certain that his civilisation is disintegrating and must inevitably perish" (*Some Time*, vii).

Although Dahl soon put *Some Time Never* behind him, writing the book was an important step in his literary career for at least two reasons. The experience taught him that he vastly preferred to write short stories over novels. Heeding this lesson, he became a short-story specialist. The experience also gave him an opportunity to begin working through his ideas on the self-destructive aspects of human nature. Long after the publication of *Some Time Never* he remained interested in this subject. He eventually became famous for his short stories about characters who engage in unusual forms of self-destructive behavior.

# 3

# Mastering the Macabre

In the late 1940s Dahl began writing macabre short stories. Although he always came up with new and unusual plot lines, these carefully contructed stories soon began to follow a discernible pattern: seemingly respectable characters are confronted with peculiar problems or opportunities and respond by committing, or at least contemplating, cruel or self-destructive acts. In most of these stories Dahl used sardonic humor, implied violence, and surprise endings. Often he incorporated material that related to his own recreational pursuits, such as collecting paintings and fine wines.

As he had done with his war stories, he submitted his macabre stories to American magazines, which quickly accepted them. The *New Yorker,* often seen as the most prestigious magazine in America, published eight of these stories between 1949 and 1959. This impressive record helped establish Dahl as a major figure on the American literary scene. Building upon this reputation, Dahl brought out three important collections of his macabre stories: *Someone Like You* (1953), *Kiss Kiss* (1960), and *Switch Bitch* (1974). He published another anthology in 1977 under the title *The Wonderful Story of Henry Sugar and Six More.* Although not as well known as his three earlier collections, this anthology does include some macabre stories. He also wrote a novel entitled

*My Uncle Oswald,* which came out in 1979. This novel directly relates to two of the stories in *Switch Bitch,* but it is somewhat less macabre than most of Dahl's short stories.

## *Someone Like You*

Almost all of the 18 stories in *Someone Like You* deal with characters whose daily routines are disturbed, resulting in various types of personal crises. When first introduced, these characters usually give every appearance of being upstanding members of society. They are generally wealthy, well educated, and highly regarded by their peers. Unlike most of the pilots in Dahl's war stories, however, these characters do not behave nobly under pressure. They often experience intense feelings of confusion, fear, anger, greed, or jealousy. These feelings cloud their judgment and cause them to lose their moral bearings.

Although most of the characters in these stories find themselves in situations that test their moral fiber, the central characters in "The Soldier" and "The Wish" confront a more basic problem: they lose touch with reality. "The Soldier," the only story in the collection that directly relates to Dahl's earlier war stories, deals with a character who floats in time, unable to distinguish between the present and the past. Although the story is set in peacetime, he still thinks he hears gunfire and still ducks when planes fly overhead. His paranoia also affects his relationship with his wife. He suspects her of playing tricks on him, such as tinkering with the taps in the bathroom so that hot water comes out of the cold-water tap. He eventually becomes so tangled up in his delusions that he mistakes another woman for his wife. "The Wish" is about a boy with a very active imagination. He pretends that a multi-colored carpet in his home is a dangerous obstacle course. He imagines that the red patches are hot coals and the black patches are poisonous snakes. Pretending that the yellow parts are the only ones upon which he can safely step, he sets out to cross the carpet. In his mind this game soon becomes a life-threatening experience. His emotional reactions to the imagined dangers are the same as they would be if the coals and snakes were real. In both of these stories the characters' behavior is governed much more by their fantasies and emotions than by reality and reason.

Disturbing memories and imagined foes also haunt the central character in "Galloping Foxley." At first glance this man appears to be completely rational and businesslike. Over the 36 years that he has been working, he has developed a rigid routine, part of which involves riding the train to and from his job. He loves the predictability of his routine and is annoyed when anything varies from the norm. One day a stranger shows up at the station where he catches the train each morning, and this disturbs him a great deal. After listening to the stranger's voice, he becomes convinced that this man is Galloping Foxley, the bully who beat him when he was a schoolboy almost 50 years earlier. The memories of these beatings come flooding back, tormenting him to the point that he becomes obsessed with the stranger. He finally decides to confront his old foe, only to discover that he is completely mistaken about the man's identity. This story exemplifies a major theme that runs through many of Dahl's stories: that adherence to daily routines can give one the false appearance of psychological stability.

Mary Maloney, the main character in "Lamb to Slaughter," is a prime example of a person who at first glance seems perfectly normal. She is the wife of a police officer, and she goes to great lengths to please him. When he comes home from work she always takes his coat and fixes him a drink. The couple then sit quietly together for a little while before she prepares their dinner. On the day in which the story takes place, this routine is disturbed when the husband confesses that he is having an affair and wants a divorce. Mary responds by bashing in his head with the frozen leg of lamb that she had planned to cook for dinner. For the rest of the story she calmly and cleverly goes about averting suspicion and disposing of the murder weapon. What is so unsettling about this character is not the anger that she feels but the way in which she expresses it. She so easily makes the transition from housewife to murderer that one wonders about her mental state prior to the day she killed her husband. Perhaps she had always been a killer but had carefully hidden this aspect of her personality. The more chilling interpretation is that she is normal and that normal people, in certain circumstances, can turn into murderers.

Another Dahl character who becomes hostile under pressure is Harry Pope, the protagonist in "Poison." He is an Englishman who lives in India. His housemate, who serves as the story's narrator, comes home late one night to find Pope lying motionless in bed and looking terrified. The narrator asks what is wrong, and Pope whispers that under the covers a poisonous snake is lying asleep on his stomach. Not knowing what to do, the narrator calls the town's native doctor. The doctor hurries over and painstakingly pours chloroform through a tube, one end of which he has placed under the bedcovers, in order to make the snake unconscious. When the doctor finally turns back the covers, however, there is no snake to be seen. The doctor asks Pope if he is sure that he had actually seen a snake, and Pope responds by calling the doctor a "dirty little Hindu sewer rat."[1] The doctor shrugs off the insult and suggests that Pope simply needs a vacation, but the reader is not so ready to forgive Pope's hostility, ingratitude, and racism. It seems quite possible that the crisis with the snake brought out Pope's true personality.

In several of these stories the characters' undoings are caused not by anger or fear but by greed and competition. Two such stories are "Man from the South" and "Dip in the Pool." Both involve gambling, but the forms that the gambling takes are out of the ordinary. In "Man from the South" a young American sailor boasts that his cigarette lighter never fails to work. An elderly gentleman from South America overhears this boast and asks if the sailor is willing to "have a good bet on dis ting" (*Someone,* 42). The South American offers to give the sailor his Cadillac if the lighter works 10 times in a row; if the lighter fails this test, the South American proposes, he will chop off one of the sailor's little fingers. Although it is obvious that the South American is mentally unbalanced, the sailor's competitive spirit and desire for the fancy car cause him to ignore his better judgment, and he accepts the bet.

The self-destructive behavior exhibited by the sailor, though certainly dramatic, pales in comparison to the actions taken by

the central character in "Dip in the Pool." While crossing the Atlantic on an oceanliner, this character decides to participate in a
contest sponsored by the ship's crew. The contest involves guess-
ing the number of miles the ship travels each day, and the winner
will collect a considerable sum of money. The protagonist guesses
a low figure, assuming that an unexpected storm they have encountered will delay the ship. The storm blows over, however, and
the ship resumes its normal speed. Determined to win the contest,
he concocts a daring plan to slow down the ship. His idea is to
jump overboard and then call for help, forcing the ship to stop so
that he can be rescued. He makes sure that a woman passenger
sees him as he deliberately falls overboard, but it never occurs to
him that she might not sound the alarm. His downfall, like the
downfalls of many other Dahl characters, comes about because he
allows his emotions and egotism to overwhelm his ability to think
clearly.

Most of the remaining stories in the collection deal with characters who belong to society's artistic and intellectual elite. The conventional wisdom is that highly cultured people are wiser and
more compassionate than those with less education, but this generalization does not apply to Dahl's characters. If anything, his
aesthetes and art collectors are even more devious and cruel than
his other characters. Although they give the appearance of being
considerate, they are fully capable of committing evil and sometimes violent deeds.

In "Taste" Dahl uses two affluent characters to satirize the idea
that high culture is an ennobling force. One of the characters, a
successful stockbroker named Mike Schofield, does not want to be
known as a crass businessman. For this reason he is trying "to
become a man of culture, to cultivate a literary and aesthetic
taste, to collect paintings, music, books, and all the rest of it"
(*Someone,* 5). The other character, an independently wealthy man
named Richard Pratt, is a well-known collector and connoisseur of
fine wines. Schofield sees Pratt as an ideal role model and feels
honored when Pratt deigns to dine with him.

At a dinner party for Pratt and a few other guests, Schofield
serves a wine from an obscure vineyard, and he is sure that Pratt

will never guess the vineyard from which the wine originated. When Schofield bets Pratt that he cannot identify the wine's breed and vintage, Pratt accepts, but rather than bet a case of wine, as Schofield proposes, Pratt suggests that they play for much higher stakes. If he wins, the prize that Pratt wants is Schofield's daughter, but if he loses, he agrees to sign over both of his houses. When it becomes clear that Pratt is serious, Schofield begins to realize that Pratt is not the upstanding aristocrat he had always imagined. As the contest concludes, Pratt's gentlemanly facade is stripped away, and he is revealed to be an unscrupulous cad, while Schofield's efforts to become as cultured as Pratt dramatically backfire.

Pratt is only one of several characters whose genteel facades break apart. The central character in "Nunc Dimittis" sees himself as a witty "man of culture" who is "adored by his many friends" (*Someone,* 219). Upon learning that the woman he is dating finds him boring, he becomes hurt and angry. Consumed with a desire to get even, he devises a novel way to embarrass the woman, but in the process of implementing his plan he loses his manners, his dignity, and his friends' good will. In "Skin" one of the characters is a well-known art dealer. In the presence of wealthy art collectors, he gives every appearance of being a perfect gentleman, but when he is associating with an impoverished owner of a valuable painting, a more sinister side of his personality emerges. Similarly, the protagonist in "Neck" seems to be a mild man who spends his time collecting art and trying to appease his domineering wife, but when presented with an opportunity to rid himself of this woman, his mild demeanor begins to crack.

The characters in this collection, whether they are highly cultured art collectors or down-to-earth businessmen, tend to be essentially self-centered. They may be married or have other long-term relationships, but they generally do not concern themselves very much about the happiness and welfare of anybody but themselves. Although this tendency is not always evident at first, it becomes obvious when the characters are placed in crisis situations. There are, however, two notable exceptions. One is Klausner, the main character in "The Sound Machine," and the other is

Claud, a character who appears in four loosely related stories known collectively as "Claud's Dog."

Klausner is an eccentric inventor who is fascinated with the sounds that the human ear cannot hear. He sets out to build a machine that will enable him to hear extremely high-pitched sounds, and after much tinkering he succeeds. With the aid of his sound machine he accidentally discovers that flowers emit sounds when they are being picked. This discovery leads him to conduct an experiment. He hooks up his machine and then listens while he strikes a tree with an axe. The sound he hears is filled with such agony that he immediately regrets his experiment and attempts to alleviate the tree's pain. Klausner's actions seem insane to the other major character in the story, but to the reader they seem admirable. Unlike most of Dahl's other characters, who are driven by fear or jealousy or greed, Klausner is motivated by an honorable desire to learn more about the natural world. Also to his credit, he does not let his quest for knowledge overwhelm his feelings of compassion for those in pain.

Claud is a young gas-station attendant who grew up in a rural working-class environment. He does not know much about high culture, but he is very knowledgeable about certain subjects, greyhound racing being foremost among them. Claud gives the initial appearance of being an uncouth schemer. When his prospective father-in-law asks about his plans for the future, Claud launches into a nauseatingly graphic description of a maggot factory that he might establish. Although Claud's maggot factory almost sounds viable, his most carefully thought-out scheme involves greyhound racing. He owns two greyhounds that look identical, but one runs much more quickly than the other. His plan is to enter the slow dog in numerous races. Then, after the bookmakers decide that the dog has no chance of ever winning, Claud intends to substitute the faster dog and bet heavily on its performance.

There is, however, more to Claud than his clever schemes. In his dealings with his girlfriend and her father, Claud shows an endearing combination of tenderness and strength. He treats her kindly and clearly cares about her happiness. For her sake he tries to get along with her stern and rigid father. But when the father attempts to browbeat Claud it becomes obvious that Claud cannot be easily intimidated. Claud's kind but forceful personality also comes through in his dealings with the greyhounds. As an experienced dog trainer, he knows all about the cruel tricks that other trainers use to speed up or slow down their dogs, but he passionately condemns these practices. Although he has few qualms about cheating, he cannot abide cruelty. He showers his own dogs with affection and wishes that other dog owners and trainers would do the same. Thus, even though Claud is crude and a bit dishonest, he still possesses an underlying sense of dignity.

When compared to the other characters in the collection, Klausner and Claud not only seem less self-centered; they also seem less concerned about their social standing. What other people may think of their actions is of little importance to these men. They are not trying to impress people with their specialized knowledge or collections of rare objects, nor are they trying to affect highly cultured images. Both men are genuinely interested in the subjects they pursue, and they resist societal pressure to give up their interests. They also take a skeptical view of societal rules and conventions. They do not go out of their way to break rules, but they often ignore them. In many ways, Klausner and Claud seem to be following the advice of the English essayist William Hazlitt, who advocated "living in the world, as in it, not of it." By distancing themselves from society, these two characters manage to avoid some of the traps that trip up most of Dahl's other characters.

Taken together, the stories in *Someone Like You* suggest that the modern world is not nearly as civilized as it makes itself out to be. Most of Dahl's characters, though they at first appear to be paragons of civilization, are really savages at heart. An element of savagery can also be found in most of the social and cultural institutions that figure in Dahl's stories. This theme, however, received little attention from the critics who reviewed the book. Instead, they focused on Dahl's writing style and the construction of his plots.

In a rave review published in the *New York Times Book Review,* James Kelly compared Dahl to Saki and O. Henry and commended Dahl for having "a masterful hand with nuance and an ability to keep the reader off balance through sheer astonishment."[2] William Penden, who reviewed the book for *Saturday Review*, seemed especially impressed with Dahl's use of "the principle of contrast." Penden argued that "these bizarre stories are heightened by the matter-of-fact and realistic method with which the author approaches his surprise endings."[3] One of the few negative reviews appeared in *Time*. The author of this review described Dahl's plots as "anecdotal gimmicks" and said that his characters are underdeveloped, but even this critic commented favorably on Dahl's technique: "Dahl is an adroit craftsman who knows how to make the unlikely seem probable. He builds long bridges of suspense, then skillfully carries his stories across to his predetermined points."[4]

In addition to garnering postive reviews, *Someone Like You* won Dahl his first major literary honor. In 1954 the Mystery Writers of America presented Dahl with their Edgar Allen Poe Award. All this acclaim helped the book succeed in the marketplace. Although short-story anthologies generally do not sell as well as novels, *Someone Like You* achieved best-seller status and remained in demand many years after its initial publication.

## Kiss Kiss

In February 1960 Knopf published *Kiss Kiss*, a collection of 11 of Dahl's stories. Four of these stories had never before been published. Of the remaining stories, four had originally appeared in the *New Yorker*, while the others had first seen print in either *Esquire*, *Nugget*, or *Playboy*. Like the stories in *Someone Like You*, those in *Kiss Kiss* have tightly woven plots, macabre elements, and surprise endings. Also, many of the characters in *Kiss Kiss* have much in common with the quirky characters from Dahl's earlier stories. In fact, two of the *Kiss Kiss* stories feature Claud, the same character who figures in several of the stories in *Someone Like You*. There is, however, a major difference between the two collections. Most of the stories in *Kiss Kiss* focus on tense and unhappy relationships between men and women, whereas just a few of the stories in *Someone Like You* treat this theme.

Among the stories in *Kiss Kiss,* only three do not involve conflicts between the sexes. Two of these—"Parson's Pleasure" and "The Champion of the World"—are about the experiences of Claud and his rustic friends. In "Parson's Pleasure" Claud and his neighbors are the target of a wealthy antique dealer who tries to con them into selling a rare Chippendale commode that Claud's neighbors happen to own. Claud and his neighbors are drawn in by this fast-talking con artist, but because they believe his lies and act accordingly, they unwittingly foil his scheme. The underlying class conflict in "Parson's Pleasure" is even more evident in "The Champion of the World." In this story Claud introduces a friend to the art of poaching pheasants. Together they set out to capture nearly all of the pheasants that live on a vast tract of land owned by a wealthy sausage manufacturer. They want to accomplish this feat before the sausage manufacturer has his pheasant-hunting party, an annual event to which only the rich and the titled are invited. In both of these stories arrogant members of the upper class discover that they do not have total control over the country folk whom they so despise.

The other story in this collection that does not involve a conflict between the sexes is "Pig." This strange parable is about a boy who lives with his aunt on an isolated farm in the mountains of Virginia. The aunt is determined to preserve the boy's innocence, so she shelters him from the evils of the world. She keeps him out of school, raises him to be a vegetarian, and never takes him to town. When the boy is 17 his aunt dies, and he is suddenly forced to enter society. He does not, however, have the survival skills necessary to cope with life away from the farm, and he quickly meets a grisly end. In some ways this character is similar to Claud: they both have rural roots, limited educations, and pleasant dispositions. But Claud at least knows how society works. The boy in "Pig" is so naive and trusting that he cannot distinguish between good and bad advice. His innocence, in a sense, prevents him from taking control over his own life.

In the other stories a member of one sex is usually trying to control a member of the opposite sex. This pattern is first seen in the collection's lead story, a haunting tale entitled "The Landlady." Modeled after traditional ghost stories, "The Landlady" features a mysterious bed-and-breakfast establishment, a peculiar woman who owns the place, and a young man who decides to spend the night there. Shortly after entering the house, the young man learns that only two people have ever signed the guest book and that several years have elapsed since the last guest signed in. When he asks the landlady about the men whose names are in the guest book, she informs him that "they're on the fourth floor, both of them together."[5] She also informs him that she has a passionate interest in taxidermy. The young man begins to suspect that something is not quite right, but his fate is already sealed.

What sets the landlady apart from many other murderers is her attitude toward her victims. She does not really think of them as being dead. By preserving their bodies, she is able to transform her victims into lifelike dolls. She visits them, provides them with a room, and takes pleasure in examining their physiques. For her these corpses are better company than live men, in part because she can exercise total control over them. The landlady, in other words, controls the men in her life by literally reducing them to possessions.

Mary Pearl, one of the central characters in "William and Mary," also gains control over the man in her life, but only after a most extraordinary turn of events. For most of her adult life Mary's stodgy and domineering husband had dictated her every move. He had not let her smoke, watch television, or participate in decision making. As the story opens she is under the impression that her husband has recently died, and she is beginning to enjoy her newfound freedom. She learns, however, that shortly before her husband's body had failed, he had agreed to participate in a medical experiment. As a result of this experiment his brain and one of his eyes continue to function normally, although they are detached from the rest of his body. At first she is quite taken aback by this strange news, but after seeing him in his altered state she realizes that she prefers him this way and decides to take him home with her. "From now on," she tells her bodiless husband, "you are going to do just exactly what Mary tells you" (*Kiss*, 53).

Mary's desire to bring her husband home is partially motivated by revenge. This becomes obvious when she deliberately smokes a cigarette within his sight, even though she knows that he disapproves of smoking. Revenge, however, is not the only reason she wants to take control over her husband's life. She feels that the scientist who conducted the experiment does not know how to care for her husband. She points out, for example, that the newspaper that the scientist had placed before her husband's eye is not the one that her husband likes to read, and she insists that it be replaced with his favorite newspaper. It is not that she wants to make her husband miserable; it is just that she wants to be in charge. Mary and her husband both care for each other, but neither is capable of treating the other as an equal.

Unlike Mary and her husband, Mr. and Mrs. Foster, the central characters in "The Way Up to Heaven," care little about each other's welfare. These elderly and extremely well-to-do Americans live in a mansion in New York City. The mansion is so big that they are able to avoid each other most of the time, but when they are together they become tense. Mr. Foster exacerbates this tension by playing upon his wife's fear of arriving late to appointments. He seems to take a perverse pleasure in delaying their departures from the mansion until the last possible minute, knowing full well that this behavior makes his wife extremely agitated. During the course of the story Mr. Foster nearly succeeds in making his wife miss her long-planned flight to Paris. In the end, though, she not only catches the flight; she also wins the undeclared war that they have been quietly waging. Her victory proves that she is more than a match for her husband when it comes to the cunning use of passive aggression. For Mr. and Mrs. Foster the impulse to control the other is rooted in aggression and is not associated with possessive or protective feelings.

The other couples in the *Kiss Kiss* stories are not quite as combative as Mr. and Mrs. Foster, but they certainly do not have ideal marriages. Mr. and Mrs. Bixby in "Mrs. Bixby and the Colonel's Coat" treat each other in a civil manner, but both are hiding extramarital affairs. Edward and Louisa in "Edward the Conqueror" seem to have a good marriage at first, but it is undermined by Edward's jealousy and narrow-mindedness. In "Genesis and Catastrophe: A True Story," Alois and Klara Hitler (the parents of Adolf Hitler) have a rocky marriage that has been strained to its limits by the deaths of their first three children. Albert and Mabel Taylor, the major characters in "Royal Jelly," have a loving relationship, but even they are pulled apart when their newborn daughter refuses to eat. Without exception, the couples in these stories do not have open and honest relationships. At least one member of each couple uses intimidation, deception, or outright violence in an attempt to control his or her spouse.

"Georgy Porgy," the remaining story in the collection, focuses on a young clergyman named George. Although this story is not about marital dynamics, it does deal with male-female relationships. In part because of a traumatic childhood experience, George has an inordinate fear of sexuality. He is uncomfortable when women touch him, and the idea of being kissed by a woman repulses him. Not knowing how disturbed George is, some of the single women in his parish occasionally flirt with him in a playful way, and this drives George to the verge of insanity. Toward the end of the story an attractive woman propositions George, precipitating his psychological breakdown and subsequent institutionalization.

The issue of control plays a major role in "Georgy Porgy," just as it does in most of the other stories in *Kiss Kiss*. In this story, however, the major character is not trying to control other characters; he is simply trying to control himself. Unable to understand or tolerate his sexual impulses, he tries to repress them at all times. It is clear that he is a clergyman largely because it is an occupation that is often associated with celibacy. But try as he might, he cannot gain total control over this part of his personality. His refusal to accept his sexuality eventually causes him to lose control over all the other aspects of his life. In a way George's struggle to control his sexuality is similar to the experiences that many Dahl characters have when they attempt to control the lives of other people. The drive to be in control not only makes it difficult for all of these characters to accept other people and care for their welfare; it also often results in their isolation and self-destruction.

Like the critics who reviewed *Someone Like You,* most of the reviewers who wrote about *Kiss Kiss* praised Dahl for his ingenious plots and his careful use of details, but they paid little attention to the ideas and themes that underlie his stories. Some of the more thoughtful reviewers, however, did comment on Dahl's characters. The reviewer for *Time* made special note of "Dahl's gallery of females." Intrigued by the deceptiveness of these characters' gentle demeanors, this reviewer described them as "lovely ladies, indeed, but heaven help the poor man who falls into their clutches."[6] In a review published in the *New York Times Book Review* Malcolm Bradbury commended Dahl for knowing "his characters inside out." Dahl's characters, Bradbury observed, "are usually ignoble: he knows the dog beneath the skin, or works hard to find it."[7] Picking up on this point, the reviewer for the *Times Literary Supplement* wrote, "Where Mr. Dahl differs from the common run of spine-chillers is in the verisimiltude of his caricature of human weakness, . . . revealing a social satirist and moralist at work behind the entertaining fantast."[8]

The suggestion that Dahl's characters should be seen as caricatures of human frailty is certainly valid. Although the reviewer for the *Times Literary Supplement* did not elaborate on this point, it lies at the core of Dahl's stories. Like any good caricaturist, Dahl exaggerates particular aspects of his characters' personalities in order to focus the reader's attention on traits and behavior patterns that might otherwise go unnoticed. In most of the *Kiss Kiss* stories these traits and behavior patterns are associated with the tensions between men and women. Although exaggerated, these tensions are present in many marriages and other male-female relationships. Thus, even though Dahl's characters may not be realistic, they are still drawn from real life.

## Switch Bitch

Dahl's next major short-story collection, a volume entitled *Switch Bitch,* came out in 1974, some 14 years after the publication of

*Kiss Kiss.* During the intervening period Dahl mostly wrote children's books, but he also wrote four adult stories. These stories, which originally appeared in *Playboy,* make up *Switch Bitch.* In one way or another all of these stories deal with sexuality, a subject that Dahl seldom addressed in his earlier stories. He was well aware of this new development in his writing and commented on it during an interview. "For twenty-five years," he noted, "I was able to write stories that were untarnished by sexual undertones of any kind. But now, in my late middle age, they're riddled with sex and copulation. What, I wonder, is the reason for this?"[9] Regardless of the reason he began writing about sexuality, Dahl succeeded in exploring some of the psychological dimensions of the subject without graphically depicting any sexual acts.

Two of the stories in *Switch Bitch*—"The Visitor" and "Bitch"— feature a character named Oswald Hendryks Cornelius. This character is the quintessential playboy. His tremendous wealth enables him to concentrate on various leisure-time pursuits, such as collecting spiders and scorpions, traveling to exotic locales, and seducing women. For all his worldliness, however, Oswald actually has quite a lot in common with George, the timid clergyman in "Georgy Porgy." Both men are fastidious about their appearance, worried about their health, and passionate about their hobbies. Both men also have strong sex drives but are afraid of having long-term relationships with women. The major difference between the two characters is that George tries to repress his sexuality, whereas Oswald has sex with many women but refuses to associate with them afterward.

Oswald is introduced in "The Visitor," a story that first saw print in the May 1965 issue of *Playboy.* This tale begins with a little frame story in which the narrator explains how he came into possession of his Uncle Oswald's diaries and then goes on to say that he has decided to publish the final entry that his uncle wrote. The rest of the story is told from Oswald's point of view and concerns his experiences during a trip across the Sinai Desert. Halfway between Cairo and Jerusalem his car breaks down, and he is forced to stay at a small gas station in the middle of the desert until the needed part is delivered. A wealthy Arab happens to come by and offers to let Oswald spend the night at his place, which is located on an oasis. Oswald accepts the invitation, and together they drive to the Arab's castlelike home.

The Arab introduces Oswald to his wife and a young woman who is his daughter. Oswald, of course, tries to seduce both women, but neither of them seems willing to arrange a rendez-vous. Disappointed, Oswald retires for the evening. In the middle of the night a woman slips into his room, and Oswald readily agrees to her sexual agenda. Since the room is totally dark and she never says a word, Oswald is not sure whether she is the mother or the daughter. Eventually, he discovers that neither of those women is the one who had come into his room. His mysteri-ous bed companion, he is shocked to learn, is a woman whom he would never have touched had he known anything about her.

As is often the case with Dahl's characters, arrogance contrib-utes to Oswald's downfall. His condescending attitude toward women and his determination to have sex with whomever he chooses blind him to the possibility that he might simply be a pawn in somebody else's game. On another level, though, his downfall can be seen as a testament to the power of the libido. Normally, Oswald is an incredibly cautious man. He insists that his water be boiled for eight minutes before he drinks it, and he refuses to eat off of a plate unless it is spotless. He distrusts prac-tically everything that is said to him, and he avoids all contact with people who are ill. Only one thing will cause him to suspend his customary caution, and that is his sexual desire. This one weakness, however, is enough to bring about his highly ironic ruin.

Although written a number of years after the initial appearance of "The Visitor," "Bitch" takes place about five years earlier than the first Oswald story. In this story Oswald hooks up with an olfactory chemist who hopes to create a women's perfume that would affect men in the same way that the scent produced by female dogs in heat affects male dogs. Oswald agrees to under-write the chemist's research in return for half of the profits that might result from the new perfume. After much work the chemist succeeds, and he and Oswald decide to call the perfume Bitch. The chemist, though, dies before he has a chance to write down the formula for the perfume, and Oswald is left with nothing but a tiny vial of the precious liquid. Oswald decides to use the perfume in an attempt to embarrass the president of the United States during an appearance on national television. Although the scheme is carefully planned, it backfires, and Oswald becomes the victim of his own plotting.

"Bitch" is primarily a humorous story containing many ribald scenes and concluding with an uproarious climax. Nevertheless, it has some serious implications about the relationship between sexuality and human evolution. These implications are hinted at when the chemist explains the biological principles involved in creating his perfume. He claims that "primitive man . . . retained the ape-like characteristic of jumping on any right-smelling female he ran across," but this trait was "suppressed" as the result of the emergence of "higher civilisations."[10] It is the chemist's contention that this trait still exists and can be brought out with the right stimulus. The chemist's theory, though a bit fanciful, is based on the plausible assumption that modern people still have much in common with their less-civilized ancestors and that certain sexual stimuli can cause modern people to lose their civilized attributes and devolve into amoral animals who care only about satisfying their instinctive drives. This idea serves as the story's foundation and is in keeping with Dahl's rather cynical view of civilization.

"The Great Switcheroo" is very similar in tone to "Bitch," but instead of chronicling the sexual exploits of a worldly playboy, it deals with the restlessness of two suburban husbands. Vic, the narrator of the story, and Jerry, Vic's neighbor and best friend, each want to have sex with the other's wife, but neither wants to jeopardize his marriage. They therefore decide to switch places in the middle of the night, make love to the other's wife, and then go back to their proper beds before dawn. It is a complicated plot and involves much planning, but they succeed in pulling it off. In the process, however, Vic makes some disconcerting discoveries about his marriage and his abilities as a lover. He had expected to feel exhilarated after his secret encounter, but instead he feels resentful and inadequate.

What happens to Vic is similar to what happens to Oswald in "Bitch." Both characters concoct intricate and amusing schemes that end up backfiring. Their stories, however, conclude on slightly different notes. Whereas the backfiring of Oswald's plan strikes the reader as a funny plot twist, Vic's fate seems a bit more poignant. The reason for this is that Oswald is only gambling with his pride, but Vic is risking his marriage. Even though Vic is interested in extramarital sex, he still cares about his wife, and she clearly cares about him. In fact, if not for their inability to satisfy each other sexually, they could have a happy marriage.

The most poignant story in *Switch Bitch* is "The Last Act." This story is about a middle-aged woman named Anna who is attempting to cope with life after her husband's death in an automobile accident. Anna and her husband had the most loving relationship of any couple in Dahl's stories. While her husband was alive she felt happy and fulfilled, but her happiness had instantly dissolved when she learned of his death. For a long time Anna contemplates suicide and even goes so far as setting the date, but at the last minute a friend asks for her help in running an adoption agency. Once she starts working her life stabilizes, and she decides not to go through with her suicide plans. Her emotional state gradually improves as the months pass, but she still deeply misses her husband and often experiences bouts of melancholy. Her psychiatrist suggests that she find a lover, but the idea seems like an act of betrayal to her, and she does not want to pursue it. She does, however, look up her old high-school boyfriend while she is in Dallas on a business trip, and they eventually go to her hotel room and have sex. Although her psychiatrist had said that resuming her sex life would be a positive step, Anna is devastated by the experience. Her defenses break down, her anguish resurfaces, and her self-destructive impulses become irresistible.

"The Last Act," though it differs in tone from the other stories in the collection, is similar to them in terms of its underlying theme. Like Oswald and Vic, Anna finds out that satisfying her sexual urges can sometimes result in a loss of self-control. At other times in her life this would not have posed a major problem, but during the time in which the story is set she needs all of the self-control that she can muster. For Anna, as well as for Oswald and Vic, sexuality is a powerful and unpredictable force. It is certainly a source of pleasure for these characters, but it also causes them to make self-destructive decisions.

Most of the critics who reviewed *Switch Bitch* seemed a bit uncomfortable with Dahl's treatment of human sexuality. Some accused him of taking the subject too lightly, while others criticized him for being too serious. Among those who wanted Dahl to be more serious was J. D. O'Hara. In a review published in *New Republic* O'Hara focused on the relationship between sexuality and evilness in Dahl's stories. O'Hara pointed out that Dahl's characters generally do not concern themselves with moral questions when they are pursuing their sexual desires, but neither are they truly villainous. O'Hara disapproved of this and explained why in the review: "Dahl substitutes for real and dangerous evil a cartoon version of it, safely incredible or at least safely removed from our everyday lives. . . . Since we can't believe in these things, the evilness in the story is presumably neutralized for us. As *Playboy* neutralizes pornograghy with an airbrush, so Dahl sweetens nastiness into mild amusement."[11] Richard P. Brickner, a reviewer for the *New York Times Book Review,* disagreed with O'Hara. He liked Dahl's humorous approach to sexuality. This type of literature, he wrote, "is for fun." Brickner, however, disliked the serious side of some of the stories, especially the touch of tragedy in "The Last Act." In Brickner's opinion, the story's tragic elements spoil the pleasure of reading the story.[12] What these reviewers seemed to miss is that Dahl's stories are intended to produce conflicting responses. In Dahl's fiction evil actions often come across as both appalling and amusing, and humor often coexists with tragedy.

## The Wonderful Story of Henry Sugar and Six More

Of all the anthologies of Dahl's writings, *The Wonderful Story of Henry Sugar and Six More* is the most eclectic. Published in 1977, this collection includes four stories, two autobiographical pieces, and an essay about a farmer in England who finds a stash of Roman artifacts buried in his field. In pulling together this collection

Dahl tried to select material that he thought teenagers would like. It is important to note, however, that most of the selections were originally written with an adult audience in mind. The four stories in the collection exhibit many of the macabre qualities found in Dahl's other short stories, but they tend to have more upbeat endings and make more extensive use of fantasy elements.

Two of the stories, "The Boy Who Talked with Animals" and "The Swan," deal with children who have special relationships with animals. In "The Boy Who Talked with Animals" some Jamaican fishermen capture a giant sea turtle and are about sell it to the local hotel owner, who plans to have it butchered and cooked. A crowd of vacationing adults are eagerly watching the preparations to kill the turtle when a young boy suddenly runs up and throws his arms around the turtle's neck. The boy manages to save the turtle, and in the process the two form a bond that is far stronger than that between the boy and his parents. In "The Swan" two teenage bullies torment a younger boy to such an extent that the boy's life is in jeopardy. Still, the boy, who is an avid bird-watcher, is more concerned about the fate of a swan that the bullies want to kill than he is about his own safety. The bullies decide to destroy both the boy and the swan, but they do not quite succeed. Cruelty plays a major role in both of these stories, but compassion plays an even bigger role.

The other two stories in the collection are about men who develop extraordinary skills in order to swindle people. In "The Hitchhiker" the story's narrator gives a ride to a scruffy-looking man. Eventually, the narrator learns that his passenger is one of the most talented pickpockets in the world. He is so good, in fact, that he calls himself a "fingersmith." The narrator expresses an interest in the pickpocket's special abilities, and the pickpocket gladly demonstrates by removing numerous articles from the narrator, including his belt, his watch, and one of his shoelaces, all without the narrator realizing that anything is missing. The pickpocket has no intention of keeping these things; he just wants to demonstrate his skills to an appreciative audience. The central character in "The Wonderful Story of Henry Sugar" develops an even more amazing skill than the pickpocket's. Henry Sugar studies yoga in order to learn how to see through cards. After spending three years perfecting this skill, he starts visiting casinos. His special ability enables him to win vast amounts of money, but he discovers that money no longer means as much to him as it did before he started studying yoga. In these stories the tremendous effort and discipline that go into acquiring a rare skill serve as mitigating forces in the lives of two characters who at least initially seem rather unsavory.

The book received mostly favorable notices, but a number of reviewers felt that it was a mistake to market it as a children's book. The reviewer for *Horn Book,* for example, praised Dahl for capturing a "feeling for the uncanny and for the venality—even viciousness—of human nature," but felt that young readers would be disappointed to learn that only two of the selections include child characters.[13] Similarly, the reviewer for the *Washington Post Book World* highly recommended the book for adult readers but felt that children would be interested in just a few of the selections.[14]

## *My Uncle Oswald*

In the late 1970s Dahl began working on another story about the exploits of Oswald Hendryks Cornelius, the same character who figures in two of the stories in *Switch Bitch.* This time he intended to write a purely humorous short story. As he told a reporter from *Publishers Weekly,* however, his short story grew into a novel entitled *My Uncle Oswald:* "I didn't set out to write a novel. The story just went on a bit and I thought it was fun."[15] The book was first published in England in 1979 by Michael Joseph, a London publishing firm. *Playboy* published an excerpt from it in January 1980, and a few months later Knopf brought out the first American edition of the book.

Like the earlier Oswald stories, *My Uncle Oswald* is presented as an extract from Oswald's diaries. Thus, all but the first two pages of the book are told from Oswald's point of view. The story, which takes place between 1912 and 1919, describes Oswald's adventures as a young man in search of a fortune. The book naturally divides into two sections. In the first half Oswald accidentally discovers that a rare insect called the Sudanese Blister Beetle works incredibly well as an aphrodisiac. He travels to the Sudan, where he purchases five pounds of powder made out of these beetles. He then uses this powder to manufacture pills, which he sells at a tremendous profit. In the second half of the book he and a beautiful female accomplice named Yasmin Howcomely travel around Europe collecting sperm from various kings and geniuses. It is Oswald's intention to sell the sperm to wealthy women who want to have a child by one of the famous donors. In the end he encounters an unexpected problem that prevents him from selling much sperm, but he still manages to become a millionaire.

The book's most humorous scenes pertain to the sperm-collecting process, which follows a peculiar pattern. Oswald and Yasmin select a name from their list of kings and geniuses. Yasmin then visits the targeted man and gives him a chocolate that contains a dose of Oswald's powerful aphrodisiac. After nine minutes the aphrodisiac takes effect, and the man is consumed with a desire to have sex with Yasmin. She always cooperates, but only after he puts on a condom. The reactions that the men have to Yasmin and the aphrodisiac make for some humorous scenes. Some of the men, such as Freud and Einstein, try to analyze what is happening to them. Others, such as George Bernard Shaw and King Haakon of Norway, put up resistance. Almost all of them, though, lose their inhibitions, their dignity, and ultimately their sperm. These scenes evoke the kind of response that people usually have to Hans Christian Andersen's story about the emperor who parades around without his clothes. There is something inherently funny about watching dignified people in undignified situations. Because of the repetitive nature of these scenes, however, they gradually lose their humorous appeal.

Another problem with the book is that it focuses on a static character. Oswald never grows or changes, and this tends to make him less interesting, despite his eccentricities. Fortunately, Yasmin, the book's most important secondary character, does change.

She, like Oswald, is something of a stereotype of the promiscuous dilettante, but she eventually transcends this image. When she is first introduced she shares Oswald's attitude toward sexuality. She enjoys sexual intercourse but sees it as a purely physical act. Over the course of the story she begins to realize that intercourse can also be a meaningful experience, one that can be emotionally as well as physically moving. She also begins to realize that relationships can encompass more than sexuality. Because of these changes in her attitude toward sexuality, she becomes increasingly reluctant to play her role in the sperm-gathering operation. As she tells Oswald toward the end of the book, "The fun's wearing off. . . . In the beginning it was a lark. Terrific joke. But now all of a sudden I seem to have had enough. . . . I think my romping days are over."[16]

Unlike the stories in *Switch Bitch, My Uncle Oswald* does not have much of a serious side. To quote from Dahl, the book is a "jokey . . . send-up."[17] Nevertheless, the way in which sexuality is treated in the book has some parallels in the *Switch Bitch* stories. In *My Uncle Oswald,* as well as in "The Visitor" and "Bitch," the urge to satisfy sexual desires is presented as an overpowering drive. Characters from all of these stories make rash decisions, or become susceptible to manipulation, while they are in a state of sexual arousal. Some interesting parallels can also be seen when comparing Yasmin to Vic from "The Great Switcheroo" and Anna from "The Last Act." These three characters all discover that having sex can produce unexpected emotional reactions. In one way or another they all learn that their sexual urges are sometimes in conflict with their emotional needs. Thus, for these characters, the act of intercourse, though it may relieve some sexual tension, results in increased emotional tension.

*My Uncle Oswald,* like *Switch Bitch,* received mixed reviews. Mollie Hardwick, who disliked the book, dismissed it as a "repetitious schoolboy joke,"[18] and David Cook, a reviewer for *New Statesman,* faulted the book for its portrayal of women and for featuring a "dislikeable hero."[19] But the book also had its defenders. In a review published in the *New Republic* Rhonda Koenig called the book a "snappy burlesque of sex novels and sex" and

praised Dahl for "his merry contempt for polite entertainment."[20]
Perhaps the most eloquent defense of the book appeared in the
*New York Times Book Review.* The reviewer, Vance Bourjaily, compared the book to an after-dinner drink: "The tone is that of a
gentleman telling ribald anecdotes to his male guests after dinner. The leer is civilized; the biographical confections make clever
use of lèse-majesté. . . . Mr. Dahl's guests are not invited to a vicarious orgy, then, nor will they hear a disguised lecture by a
wicked satirist of morals and manners. Nor, as we sip, smile and
listen, is that cognac in the snifters this time around, let alone
hemlock—it's banana and strawberry daiquiris, folks. Summer
drinks. Summer reading. To raise objections would be silly."[21]

As Bourjaily suggested, the satiric and macabre elements generally associated with Dahl's adult fiction do not play prominent
roles in *My Uncle Oswald.* There are, however, significant connections between this book and Dahl's previous stories. Oswald is
much like Dahl's other aesthetes and art collectors. They all project highly cultured personae, but this does little to temper their
basic animal drives. The portrayal of marital and other male-
female relationships in *My Uncle Oswald* also follows trends set
in earlier stories. With a few exceptions, these relationships involve deceitful behavior and manipulative power plays. Another
similarity between *My Uncle Oswald* and Dahl's other stories is
in the depiction of political and cultural leaders and institutions.
These traditional objects of respect are almost always revealed to
be either foolish or corrupt. Thus, though *My Uncle Oswald* is a
fairly lightweight novel, it still deals with the major theme that
runs through most of Dahl's adult fiction—the superficiality of
civilization.

# 4

# Switching Audiences

Following the publication of *Kiss Kiss* in 1959, Dahl decided to write for children. In explaining how he came to this decision, Dahl said, "I had been writing short stories for about fifteen years, and then I had children. I always told them stories in bed, and they started asking for some of the stories over and over. I was in New York at the time, and I didn't have a plot for a short story, so I decided to have a go at a children's book. I took some of these bed time stories and turned them into *James and the Giant Peach*" (West 1990, 63–64). This was Dahl's first children's book since writing *The Gremlins* in the early 1940s, and it marked the beginning of his career as a major children's author.

## *James and the Giant Peach*

While writing *James and the Giant Peach* Dahl tried not to imitate other children's books. As he told an interviewer, "Everyone's written about bunnies and ducks and bears and moles and rats, . . . so I searched around for . . . something new." He decided to focus on giant insects. "At first they didn't look very attractive," he admitted, but he felt that they could be made "amusing or interesting if one gave them character" (Wintle, 105). In addition to the giant insects, he included many other inventive features in the book, most notably a peach the size of a small house. He submitted the final manuscript to Knopf, who accepted it and arranged to have it illustrated by Nancy Eckholm Burkert. Knopf published the book in America in the fall of 1961. Six years later the publishing firm of Allen & Unwin brought out the first British edition of the book.

Like many traditional fairy tales, *James and the Giant Peach* is about an ill-treated child who must break away from the adults who mistreat him before he can achieve happiness. This character, whose full name is James Henry Trotter, begins life as a happy and loved boy, but at the age of four he becomes an orphan after his parents are attacked and eaten by a rhinoceros that has just escaped from the London Zoo. James then moves into a dilapidated house in the south of England, where he lives with his cruel Aunt Sponge and Aunt Spiker. For the next several years the aunts berate and often beat their young nephew, causing him to become increasingly depressed and withdrawn.

Like most traditional fairy tales, *James and the Giant Peach* is an example of low fantasy, which means that it includes fantasy elements but takes place in the real world. The first fantasy element is interjected into the story at a point when James feels like giving up on life. He is hiding behind some bushes and weeping uncontrollably when a peculiar old man comes up and gives him a bag full of tiny green objects. The old man explains to James that "there's more magic and power" in these little objects "than in all the rest of the world put together."[1] James is told that if he pours the contents of the bag into a jug of water and drinks it, he will "never be miserable again" (*James*, 10). James, though, accidentally spills the bag near a scrawny peach tree, and the little objects wriggle their way into the earth. Soon thereafter the tree, which had been barren for years, sprouts a peach.

The peach is one of the story's most important fantasy elements. In the span of a few minutes it grows from an ordinary peach into a fruit as tall as the tree to which it is attached. Determined to profit by this miraculous phenomenon, the aunts decide to sell tickets to the curious for the privilege of seeing the gargantuan fruit. Its size, though, is not the peach's only fantastic feature. As James learns when his aunts send him outside to pick up the litter left by the onlookers, there is a hole in the bottom of the peach that is big enough for a child to enter. James crawls into this opening and up through a tunnel until he reaches the center of the fruit, where the stone is located. He discovers that there is a door in the stone, and he gives it a push. It opens, and he finds himself in a room containing seven insects.

These insects constitute another of the story's fantasy elements. They are fantastically large, about the size of dogs, and they have many human qualities. They all can talk, and some of them wear articles of clothing. Four of the insects—the Ladybug, the Old-Green-Grasshopper, the Centipede, and the Earthworm—also have distinct personalities. The Ladybug is a caring, maternal figure, while the Old-Green-Grasshopper is wise and fatherlike. The Centipede is a rambunctious troublemaker, and the Earthworm is a whiny pessimist. When James first meets these insects they frighten him, but he soon overcomes his fear and becomes friends with them.

As the story progresses James and the insects go for a wild ride in the peach as it rolls over the aunts, tumbles down the hillside, and lands in the ocean. They then turn the peach into a strange airship and ride it across the Atlantic, having many adventures along the way. They finally arrive in New York City, where James is welcomed as a hero. The peach stone is transformed into a small house and placed in the middle of New York City's Central Park, and there, in true fairy-tale fashion, James lives happily ever after.

*James and the Giant Peach* can be read as simply an exciting transatlantic adventure story, but it can also be seen as a story about psychological regression. When interpreted from a psychoanalytic perspective, James's decision to enter the giant peach suggests that he wishes to escape from the harsh world and return to the security of the womb. The scene in which he climbs into the peach closely resembles a reversal of the birthing process: "The tunnel was damp and murky, and all around him was the curious bittersweet smell of fresh peach. The floor was soggy under his knees, the walls were wet and sticky, and peach juice was dripping from the ceiling. . . . He was crawling up hill now, as though the tunnel were leading straight toward the very center of the gigantic fruit" (*James*, 25).

The four major insects can also be interpreted from a psychoanalytic perspective. In many ways these insects appear to be separate aspects of James's psychological makeup. Often, during periods of regression, an individual's sense of self is fragmented. In psychological circles this is known as "splitting."[2] Splitting occurs when an individual begins to regard various aspects of his or her personality as separate entities rather than as features of a unified whole. These divisions are usually products of introjection or projection. When introjection comes into play, the individual draws upon memories of another person, usually a parent, to create an internalized representation of the person. When projection comes into play, the individual attempts to externalize certain parts of his or her personality onto another being. Both of these processes can be associated with the insects.

The Ladybug and the Old-Green-Grasshopper both appear to be products of introjection. They come across as kindly parents. They look after James, praise him when he does well, and share their knowledge with him. Unlike the cruel aunts, they provide James with the love that he so desperately needs. Although James's original parents died when he was four, they seem to live on, at least in James's mind, in the forms of these two insects.

The Centipede and the Earthworm are easily interpreted as projections of James's id. The Centipede proudly proclaims himself to be a pest. He boasts, makes trouble, sings risqué songs, and indulges in wild dances. He corresponds in some ways to Freud's notion of Eros. The Earthworm, on the other hand, is an impotent figure. He is powerless, whining, and defeated, and he constantly criticizes the Centipede. The Earthworm thus resembles Freud's conception of Thanatos, or the self-destructive aspect of the id.

Important tensions within James's psyche are played out through his interactions with these insects. As soon as James enters the peach, the Centipede takes charge of the situation. He begins ordering James about and initiating various activities. For example, before James and the insects retire for the evening, the Centipede insists that James remove the Centipede's many boots. In the morning the Centipede continues to play a dominant role. He climbs out of the peach and chews through the stem that anchors the peach to the tree, setting the peach in motion and ultimately causing it to squash the aunts. If the Centipede is viewed as a symbol of James's id, these early scenes with the Centipede indicate that James is finally allowing his aggressive impulses to surface.

The death of the aunts plays a pivotal role in the story, for it represents the first time that James admits his murderous feelings toward his caretakers. As soon as these feelings are unleashed, James's safe peach stone turns into a chaotic pit. While the peach tumbles down the hill, James and his companions are violently tossed about. In his fright James switches his allegiance from the Centipede to the Earthworm. When the peach finally comes to rest in the ocean, James and the Earthworm are wrapped around each other. This passage suggests that James fears his own aggressive impulses and seeks to deny them by embracing the impotent Earthworm. James, however, does not remain in this defeated position for more than a few moments.

Once the peach is floating peacefully in the ocean, James begins to rebuild his personality. He breaks his bond with the Earthworm and ventures out of the peach stone. Although he remains on top of the peach, he no longer seems to need the security of the womb. He is immediately confronted with numerous problems, but he bravely and cleverly solves each one. When the insects fear that they will starve, he explains that they can eat the peach. When sharks attack the peach, he manages to turn it into an airship by tying hundreds of seagulls to its stem. Each time he solves a problem, the Ladybug and the Old-Green-Grasshopper congratulate him. Their praise helps James gain a sense of self-confidence that he never had while he was living with the aunts.

As James begins to take control over his life, his relationship with the Centipede starts changing. Instead of feeling threatened by the Centipede, James grows to enjoy its jokes and sardonic songs. This change is underscored in a dramatic scene that follows one of the Centipede's wild singing sprees. The Centipede gets so carried away with his singing and dancing that he falls off the peach and lands in the ocean far below. Much to the Earthworm's disappointment, James immediately sets out to rescue the imperiled insect. After attaching himself to a strand of string, James dives into the ocean and swims around until he finds the floundering Centipede. The other insects then hoist the two of them back up to the peach. Through this symbolic acceptance of his id, James indicates that he can handle his aggressive impulses. He has realized that he need not renounce his id in order to control it.

After James safely lands in New York City, he shows many signs that he has successfully recovered from his period of regression. Although he still occasionally visits with the Ladybug, the Old-Green-Grasshopper, and the Centipede, James generally succeeds in reintegrating his fragmented personality. Moreover, his emotional disposition is vastly improved as a result of his adventures. He is no longer the miserable, guilt-ridden, withdrawn character that he was in the beginning of the story. He has become instead a cheerful boy who knows how to make friends and sustain his self-confidence. In short, he has learned how to cope with the demands of both his internal world and the external environment.

The psychological dimensions of *James and the Giant Peach* generally went unnoticed by the people who reviewed the book. Instead, they tended to focus on the story's fantasy elements. Almost without exception, they applauded Dahl's inventiveness and imagery. The reviewer for the *San Francisco Chronicle* called the book "the most original fantasy that has been published for a long time" and predicted that it "may well become a classic."[3] *Kirkus Reviews* praised Dahl for writing a "broad fantasy with all the gruesome imagery of old-fashioned fairy tales and a good measure of their breathtaking delight."[4] In a review published in the *New York Herald Tribune* M. S. Libby described the book as "a richly imaginative fantasy extremely well-told and convincingly illustrated. . . . We loved it."[5]

The book did receive one highly negative review. The author of this review, Ethel L. Heins, was a prominent children's librarian who would later become the editor of *Horn Book* magazine. Writing for the *School Library Journal*, Heins recommended against buying the book. As she stated in her tersely worded review, she objected to the book because of its "violent exaggeration of language" and the "almost grotesque characterizations of the child's aunts."[6] Although her review was overshadowed by the many positive reviews that the book received, it marked the beginning of a conflict between Dahl and some of the more traditional members of the children's-literature establishment.

## Charlie and the Chocolate Factory

Several months before *James and the Giant Peach* saw print, Lewis Nichols of the *New York Times Book Review* reported that Dahl was already at work on another children's book. According to Nichols, the book was going to be called *Charlie's Chocolate Boy,* and it would take place in a chocolate factory (Nichols, 8). While working on the initial draft of this book, Dahl experienced some crises in his family life that forced him to put the manuscript aside for a few years. When he returned to it he felt a bit dissatisfied with the story, but he was not sure that it needed a complete overhaul. He decided to show the manuscript to his nephew and see what he thought of it. As Dahl later told an interviewer, his nephew's reaction played an important role in the story's evolution: "He told me he didn't think it was much good. That shook me. Then I looked at it and I realized he was right. It wasn't very good, but I knew there was something there, so I worked and worked away at it" (Wintle, 105). In addition to revising the story, Dahl changed the title to *Charlie and the Chocolate Factory*.

Dahl gave the finished manuscript to Knopf, who published the story, with illustrations by Joseph Schindelman, in late 1964. During its first year only about 5,000 hardcover copies of the book were sold. The sales figures, though, increased dramatically over the next several years. In 1967 Allen & Unwin brought out the first British edition of the book, which resulted in even higher sales figures. Within five years of the book's initial publication its annual sales had reached 125,000 copies. In 1971 Paramount released a motion-picture version of the book under the title *Willy Wonka and the Chocolate Factory,* and this further increased the book's popularity. Throughout the 1970s and 1980s over 100,000 paperback copies were sold every year. After reviewing these combined sales figures, Kevin Nudd, a writer for *Book and Magazine Collector,* declared that "*Charlie* has established itself as one of the most enduring post-war children's books."[7]

There are many reasons that the book is so popular among young readers. It has an original and fast-moving plot about a polite boy who, along with four less-deserving children, wins an opportunity to tour a chocolate factory that has been closed to the public for 10 years. The slapstick humor and comic violence that run throughout the story also appeal to many children. The story is told in a lively and playful way; practically every page is peppered with rhymes, puns, and hyperbolic words. But perhaps the most important reasons for the book's popularity are its wondrous and sensuous setting and its unusual characters.

As its title indicates, *Charlie and the Chocolate Factory* takes place primarily in a magical confectionery, but it begins in a quasi-realistic setting. The central characters live in a contemporary industrial area that is referred to simply as "a great town."[8] Because the city's name and location are never mentioned, the setting has a sense of universality to it. It could be practically any large city in England or America. The city, however, has one distinguishing characteristic: it is the home of a chocolate factory owned by an eccentric man named Willy Wonka.

From the outside Wonka's factory looks much like any other factory, but the interior is another matter. Unbeknownst to the city's residents, most of the factory lies underground. It is a series of cheerful catacombs, full of winding tunnels and chambers of various kinds. The Chocolate Room, for example, resembles an outdoor park complete with a beautiful waterfall, only the cascading liquid is actually melted chocolate. Another chamber that figures in the story is the Inventing Room. Crammed with pipes, pots, and odd machines, the room is always a hub of activity. Although each chamber is different, a sensuous quality pervades the entire factory. It is a place where practically everything tastes, smells, and looks good.

Most of the book's characters are nearly as unusual as its setting, but the title character, Charlie Bucket, is something of an exception to this generalization. He lives in a small house with his parents and both sets of grandparents. Although the family is poverty-stricken, Charlie is still a fairly happy and well-behaved boy. His personality, however, is never fully developed. Aside from his love of chocolate bars, he has no distinguishing qualities. He is, as his name suggests, an empty container, a shell waiting to be filled. It is the reader who fills the empty space. Like many of the bland heroes of traditional fairy tales, Charlie is the sort of character upon whom the reader can easily project his or her own personality.

The other children in the story are much more memorable than Charlie, but they are not fully developed characters either. They essentially function as symbols. Agustus Gloop, an obese boy, symbolizes gluttony; Veruca Salt, a spoiled rich girl, symbolizes selfishness; Violet Beauregarde, a gum-chewing chatterbox, symbolizes mindlessness; and Mike Teavee, a television addict, symbolizes idleness. These children exhibit no distinctive traits other than the particular behavior flaws that they represent. Thus, when terrible things happen to them as a result of their reprehensible actions, the reader can take righteous pleasure in their demise without feeling the pangs of pity that one normally experiences when disasters befall real people.

Another set of characters that figure in the story are the Oompa-Loompas. They are tiny people who live and work in the factory. In the 1964 version of the book the Oompa-Loompas have black skin and are said to be pygmies from Africa. In addition to doing all of the work in Wonka's factory, they serve in much the same capacity as the chorus does in classical Greek drama. At various points they criticize the four obnoxious children or comment on events in the story. Their comments always come in the form of songs, which they sing in unison.

The most important character in the story is Willy Wonka. Although ostensibly an adult, Wonka does not conform to the typical image of an adult male. Not only is he much smaller than most men; he is also more impulsive and playful. Like the Centipede in *James and the Giant Peach,* Wonka is an aggressive character who is usually in control and almost always on the move. Of all the characters in the story, he is the most fully developed, but even he is more of a symbol than a multidimensional character. In many ways he represents the child's libidinal drives, the desires to indulge in sensuous pleasures and act out aggressive fantasies. He is free to do the things that most children only wish they could do. Thus, when children read about Wonka's antics and adventures, they experience the pleasure of seeing their own libidinal fantasies mirrored back at them.

The wildness of Dahl's setting and characters is counterbalanced by his carefully constructed and well-paced plot. In the beginning of the story Charlie's grandparents provide a tantalizing history of Wonka and his chocolate factory. They say enough to let Charlie and the reader know that the factory is a mysterious and magical place, but they do not divulge any of its secrets. The reader's sense of expectation intensifies when Wonka announces that he has hidden five golden tickets in the wrappers of his candy bars and that the children who find the tickets will be given a tour of his factory. The contest unfolds over the course of several chapters, during which the four obnoxious children are introduced. When Charlie finally finds the last golden ticket, the reader's curiosity about the factory has been piqued. This prolonged period of anticipation enhances the sense of wonderment that surrounds the factory.

The portion of the book that takes place inside the factory provides both the sensuous pleasures of a food fantasy and the thrills of an aggression fantasy. These two themes are dealt with alternately. For every chapter that is devoted to describing one of the factory's magical features, there is another chapter that details an amazing calamity experienced by one of the obnoxious children. This approach allows for the inclusion of an abundance of descriptive details without slowing down the narrative. Not only does the plot keep moving; it also builds to a satisfying climax. After four of the five children are dismissed from the tour, it is learned that Wonka intends to select the remaining child as his heir. This final surprise helps tie together the preceding events and provides the story's closure.

When *Charlie and the Chocolate Factory* first appeared it received mostly favorable reviews. Charlotte Jackson, a reviewer for the *Atlantic Monthly,* described the book as being "full of magical nonsense and uproarious situations with a tiny germ of a moral artfully inserted in each chapter."[9] In a review published in the *Saturday Review* Alice Dalgliesh called the book "an offbeat fantasy" and said that adults as well as children would enjoy its humor.[10] One of the book's most glowing reviews appeared in the *New York Times Book Review.* Aileen Pippett, the reviewer, opined that Dahl "proved in *James and the Giant Peach* that he knew how to appeal to children. He has done it again, gloriously. Fertile in invention, rich in humor, acutely observant, he depicts fantastic characters . . . and situations . . . and lets his imagination rip."[11]

Although a few of the people who initially reviewed the book expressed some minor reservations about the violence in the story, it was not until the early 1970s that the book became controversial. The controversy started when Lois Kalb Bouchard and some other critics charged that the book was racist. In 1970 Bouchard published an article entitled "A New Look at Old Favorites: *Charlie and the Chocolate Factory,*" which was reprinted a few years later in a book called *The Black American in Books for Children: Readings in Racism.* Bouchard did not accuse Dahl of "being deliberately racist," but she argued that he perpetuated racist stereotypes through his portrayal of the Oompa-Loompas. She criticized these characters' "childishness and dependency upon whites."[12] She also disliked the relationship between Wonka and the Oompa-Loompas. "As workers in the factory," Bouchard wrote, "the Black characters are exploited. The owner clicks his fingers sharply when he wants a worker to appear. The Oompa-Loompas are made to test various kinds of candies, sometimes with unfortunate effects" (Bouchard, 113).

When Dahl first heard that his book was under attack for being racist, he was a bit taken aback. He did not, however, dismiss the charges or become defensive. Instead, he gave the matter much thought and concluded that the charges were reasonable and warranted a response. During an interview Dahl explained how he had come to this conclusion. He said that when he had first created the Oompa-Loompas, he had intended them to be seen not as actual pygmies from Africa, even though he had described them as such in the book, but as "fantasy creatures" such as elves or gnomes. Elaborating on this point, he said, "I saw them as charming creatures, whereas the white kids in the book were, with the exception of Charlie, most unpleasant. It didn't occur to me that my depiction of the Oompa-Loompas was racist, but it did occur to others. They pointed out that all the workers were black." After listening to the people who made these criticisms, Dahl said that he found himself "sympathizing with them."[13] He therefore decided to revise the book. In the revised edition, published in 1973, the Oompa-Loompas are no longer black. They have long, wavy hair and come from an imaginary island called Loompaland.

The controversy surrounding *Charlie and the Chocolate Factory* diminished after Dahl made the changes to the Oompa-Loompas, but it did not disappear. Eleanor Cameron, an American children's author and occasional critic, was largely responsible for keeping the controversy alive. She accomplished this by frequently publishing criticisms of the book in children's literature journals. She first attacked the book in an article published in the October 1972 issue of *Horn Book* magazine. The next year she wrote another article for *Horn Book* in which she continued her criticism, and in 1976 she published still another piece finding fault with the book, this time in the journal *Children's Literature in Education.*

In the first of these articles Cameron called Dahl's book "one of the most tasteless books ever written for children."[14] She went on to say that she objected to the book's "phony presentation of poverty and its phony humor, which is based on punishment with overtones of sadism" (Cameron 1972, 440). She concluded her second article by asserting that the book has no literary value and is popular simply because it is "wish-fulfilling."[15] In her third article she returned to the subject of sadism. "Dahl," she wrote, "caters to the streak of sadism in children which they don't even realize is there because they are not fully self-aware and are not experienced enough to understand what sadism is."[16] She then suggested that the book harms children because it "diminishes the human spirit" and leads to a "lack of any emotion but the hyped-up one of getting kicks out of the pain and misfortune of others" (Cameron 1976, 62).

Cameron's criticisms of *Charlie and the Chocolate Factory* did not go unanswered. Soon after *Horn Book* published Cameron's first assault on the book, the editors received numerous angry letters from readers who felt compelled to defend the book. Some years later several academics also came to the book's defense, including Alasdair Campbell, one of the book's most unequivocal supporters. In an article published in the June 1981 issue of *School Librarian,* Campbell summarized Cameron's position on the book and then offered a rebuttal. He argued that Cameron ignored the book's literary value and took its fantasy elements too literally:

> I find considerable merit in the book, and I think that the undeniable anger which it has aroused is due largely to a misunderstanding of its nature. I would see *Charlie* as an amoral fairy tale in modern idiom, belonging to a tradition in which violence and ruthless punishments are taken for granted, and where deliberate stereotyping is a valid technique. I would expect child readers to realise instinctively that this is not the sort of book from which to learn about social attitudes, or in which to look for models for one's own future behavior. What one does find is an abundance of pleasure. . . . With due respect to the obviously sincere concern of Eleanor Cameron and others, I do not believe that *Charlie and the Chocolate Factory* could be in any way harmful. (Campbell, 111)

Hamida Bosmajian, an English professor at Seattle University, also defended the book. In a prize-winning essay entitled *"Charlie and the Chocolate Factory* and Other Excremental Visions," Bosmajian argued that the book might first appear to be "nothing but fun and frolic" but that it is really a complex story that deals with children's unconscious thoughts and libidinal impulses.[17] Drawing on the writings of Bruno Bettelheim and other psychoanalytic theorists, Bosmajian showed how the story relates to the issue of "oral greed." She also discussed Dahl's use of "excremental imagery" and compared this aspect of the story to passages in Dante's *Inferno* and Swift's *Gulliver's Travels* (Bosmajian, 38–39). In her conclusion she argued that the book "releases a child's anxieties about bodily functions, physical injury, and death." She stated that the book does have a dark side but insisted that it should still be made available to children. As she put it, "The range of children's literature is large enough to contain such a tale. The bookshelf must not be purged of it!" (Bosmajian, 47).

In addition to prompting response from academics, Cameron's criticisms of *Charlie and the Chocolate Factory* drew a sharp reaction from Dahl. In February 1973 *Horn Book* published a short essay by Dahl in which he replied to Cameron's first article. He expressed shocked indignation at Cameron's suggestion that the book harmed children. He explained that he had dedicated the book to his son Theo, who had been seriously injured in an accident when he was an infant. Dahl then wrote, "The thought that I would write a book for him that might actually do him harm is too ghastly to contemplate. It is an insensitive and monstrous implication."[18]

A number of years later Dahl responded in a less personal way to Cameron's charges. During an interview conducted in December 1986, he was asked why he thought Cameron and some other adults so strongly objected to *Charlie and the Chocolate Factory*. He answered by suggesting that the real reason for the conflict had to do with differing beliefs about childhood: "I think they may be unsettled because they are not quite as aware as I am that children are different from adults. Children are much more vulgar than grown-ups. They have a coarser sense of humor. They are basically more cruel. So often, though, adults judge a children's book by their own standards rather than by the child's standards" (West 1988, 74).

# 5

# Staying on Track

Shortly after finishing *Charlie and the Chocolate Factory*, Dahl wrote an essay about children's literature, which appeared in the 1 November 1964 issue of the *New York Times Book Review*. In this essay he discussed several trends that bothered him. He criticized children's authors who used restricted vocabularies, as well as those who relied on illustrations to pad their "threadbare" story lines. What concerned him most, however, was the disappearance of long fantasy stories for children. "These days," he wrote, "original works of fantasy and imagination are becoming scarcer and scarcer. Forty years ago, we had almost nothing else, and it was wonderful. Today they hardly ever appear. Instead, we are being showered with these horrible things that are called educational books" ("Let's Build," 2).

In the years following the publication of his essay, Dahl tried to counter the trendy "educational books" that he so deplored by writing a number of highly imaginative works for children between the ages of about 7 and 11. The first of these books, *Charlie and the Great Glass Elevator*, came out in 1972. A sequel to *Charlie and the Chocolate Factory*, it features several of the characters from the first book. Dahl's next book for this age group, *Danny, the Champion of the World*, was published in 1975. Although not an outright fantasy, this book is so whimsical in places that it

reads like a fantasy story. In the 1980s Dahl wrote four fully developed fantasies aimed at the 7-to-11 age group: *George's Marvelous Medicine* (1981), *The BFG* (1982), *The Witches* (1983), and
*Matilda* (1988).

## Charlie and the Great Glass Elevator

The idea of a sequel to *Charlie and the Chocolate Factory* originated with Dahl's publisher. As Dahl later recalled, he never felt
entirely comfortable with the idea: "My publishers kept screaming
for another *Charlie,* and I kept saying, 'No way, no way.' I resisted
for five or six years, but finally I said, 'All right, let's do it.' I tried
to come up with a new plot, make it different, but it wasn't much
fun writing" (West 1990, 64). Once Dahl finished the text of *Charlie and the Great Glass Elevator,* Knopf gave it to Joseph Schindelman to illustrate. *Life* published a portion of the story in its 18
August 1972 issue, and the next month Knopf released the book.

Like its predecessor, *Charlie and the Great Glass Elevator* is full
of inventive features, foremost of which is the Great Glass Elevator itself. This elevator is really a self-propelled spaceship. It is in-
destructible, highly maneuverable, and equipped to handle every
conceivable situation. It is controlled by a myriad of multicolored
buttons, which are located on all its walls. Among the book's other
inventive features are a luxury hotel that orbits around the world,
a group of space monsters called Vermicious Knids, some pills that
cause one to grow 20 years younger, and a magical liquid that can
make one age hundreds of years in the span of a second.

Unlike its predecessor, however, *Charlie and the Great Glass
Elevator* does not have a cohesive story line. It essentially consists
of two plots that are loosely spliced together. In the first half of
the book Willy Wonka, Charlie, Charlie's parents, and his four
grandparents board the elevator for a ride to the chocolate factory,
but because one of the grandmothers interrupts Wonka while he
is navigating the elevator, they end up in outer space. This sets
the stage for a farcical adventure involving astronauts, the president of the United States, and monsters from another solar system.

The second half of the book takes place in the chocolate factory, but the factory plays only a minor role in the story. This section focuses on Wonka's attempts to get Charlie's three bedridden grandparents out of bed. Wonka tells these old folks that he has invented a magical pill called Wonka-Vite. He explains that if they each swallow one of these pills they will become 20 years younger and will feel well enough to leave their beds. They become so enthusiastic about the prospect of growing younger that they take an overdose of the pills. All sorts of complications result before Wonka finally manages to set things right.

The two halves of the book differ somewhat in tone. The first part is quite satirical. Except for Wonka, all of the authority figures in this section are described in unflattering ways. The scientists and astronauts are basically incompetent, the president's advisors are a bunch of silly sycophants, and the president himself is an egocentric imbecile. Dahl satirized these characters in part because he wanted to deflate some of the mindless patriotism that is taught in American schools. He expanded on this point after an interviewer asked him why he presented the president in such a negative light:

> I just didn't like the whole political system and the way in which a President is [anointed] and the long term he lasts and the patronage he hands out everywhere. The man is treated with such tremendous respect by the children in America. There is something dangerous about the whole thing. The kids are forced to stand up and recite the pledge of allegiance every morning at school before lessons and put their hands on their hearts and all that rubbish. It really is rubbish, dangerous rubbish. Patriotism is a good thing in small doses, but it's also a rotten thing. It leads to war. (Wintle, 106)

The second half of the book is not nearly as satirical as the first half. Instead, the story takes on an absurd quality that borders on surrealism. The story begins moving in this direction when the three bedridden grandparents swallow too many Wonka-Vite pills and suddenly become 80 years younger. Two of them are turned into infants, and this leads to some very odd dialogue. For example, when the one grandparent who refrains from taking the pills witnesses the transformation of his spouse, he exclaims, "I've got a screaming baby for a wife!"[1] The most amazing transformation occurs in the grandparent who is only 78 years old when she takes the pills. She becomes minus two, which means that she must spend two years in Minusland unless Wonka is able to rescue her. Minusland is depicted as a "gray inhuman nothingness," (*Glass*, 133) a sort of "hell without heat" (*Glass*, 135). There is a mystical, almost nightmarish quality to the passages set in Minusland. Although these passages are intriguing, they seem out of keeping with the rest of the story.

The book's lack of a cohesive plot and consistent tone did not go unnoticed by the critics who reviewed it. In the *New York Times Book Review* Julia Whedon described the book as "a string of random jokes and adventures held together by that enviable British glibness of style—punning and colloquial—that sounds as if it must be good, even though it's all manner, without substance."[2] In the *Saturday Review* Karla Kuskin wrote that she liked portions of the book but found some of the passages a bit dull. She playfully suggested that Dahl must have been feeling drowsy while he was writing certain parts of the story. "When he is awake," she wrote, "everything is engaging and lively, but there are arid stretches where he seems to have fallen off from sheer boredom."[3] Almost all the reviewers pronounced the book inferior to *Charlie and the Chocolate Factory*. The negative reaction to *Charlie and the Great Glass Elevator* helped convince Dahl that he had made a mistake in agreeing to write a sequel. "I'll never do it again," he said during an interview, "no matter how much the publishers scream" (West 1990, 64).

## Danny, the Champion of the World

Although Dahl resolved never to write another sequel, he did not forswear the reuse of material from his earlier works. He saw nothing wrong with occasionally taking a snippet from one story and plugging it into another. When he began writing *Danny, the Champion of the World,* however, he did not limit himself to a snippet; he borrowed the entire plot line and most of the title from his adult story "The Champion of the World." That story, which details the adventures of two men who go pheasant poaching, appeared in the *New Yorker* in January 1959 and then in Dahl's short-story collection *Kiss Kiss* in 1960. In reworking the story into a children's book Dahl kept the setting and all of the material about pheasant poaching, but he changed the central characters into a father and his son. He also made many changes in the language and added much more background material before sending the manuscript to Knopf. In September 1975 Knopf published the book, with illustrations by Jill Bennett.

Unlike most of Dahl's other children's books, *Danny, the Champion of the World* is told in the first person. The narrator is Danny, a nine-year-old boy who was left motherless when he was four months old. He lives with his father, a man named William, in a rural area in the South of England. The father owns a small gas station, and Danny helps his father pump gas and repair cars. They live in an old gypsy caravan that is located behind the station. Although the caravan is barely big enough to hold two bunk beds and a small table, Danny does not mind the cramped quarters. One of the reasons he likes living in the caravan is that he is always near his father.

The two have a very close relationship. William is openly affectionate toward Danny and spends lots of time playing with the boy and telling him stories. William also tries to involve Danny in his work. He teaches Danny how to take apart an automobile engine and put it back together again, as well as how to drive. Danny thrives on the love and attention his father provides. He enjoys his father's company so much that he does not invite his friends to visit, because playing with them would consume time that he would otherwise spend with his father. Since Danny sees his father as being practically perfect, he is shocked when he learns that his father has a penchant for poaching pheasants.

The core of the book focuses on Danny's introduction to "the art of poaching."[4] Danny first sees poaching as outright thievery, but William convinces the boy that poaching is both an "exciting sport" (*Danny,* 29) and a way for ordinary people to strike back at the wealthy people who own the land where the pheasants live. William then tells Danny about the various techniques that poachers use to catch pheasants without firing guns. Danny soon catches his father's love of poaching. After giving the matter some thought, Danny thinks of a new and very effective way to poach pheasants. They decide to use this new method to spoil the local land baron's annual pheasant-shooting party, an event to which only rich people or those with titles are invited.

In addition to its strong plot, the story has interesting ethical implications. By presenting poaching in a positive light the story suggests that not all of society's rules are equally just. The reader gets the impression that it is not morally wrong to disobey laws that are designed solely to protect the interests of the privileged class. The story makes it clear that there are risks involved in disobeying these rules but that running a risk is not the same as being unethical. The reader also gets the impression that it is more important to practice the virtues of kindness and familial love than to follow societal rules and conventions. In a sense the story introduces children to the concept of situational ethics.

Rather than discuss the story's ethical implications, most of the critics who reviewed the book concentrated on praising the fast-moving plot and the loving relationship between William and Danny. A few reviewers, however, did comment on the characters' willingness to break laws. Philippa Pearce, who reviewed the book for the *Times Literary Supplement,* felt ambivalent about a scene in which Danny drives a car by himself. She called this scene "reprehensible," but she also found it "marvellously gripping."[5] In a review published in *Growing Point* Margery Fisher pointed out that for Dahl "the power of love" is "more important . . . than social morality."[6] Alasdair Campbell, one of the few critics who seriously addressed the ethical issues in the story, stated that some people might find the book "unacceptable because the hero and his father are triumphant poachers; and if poaching can be presented as a heroic activity, what about shoplifting or any other kind of theft?" But Campbell went on to argue that the book "is far enough into the world of make-believe for it to escape the charge of encouraging crime—although the author certainly does intend to promote a critical attitude towards land-owning and game-shooting" (Campbell, 111–12).

## George's Marvelous Medicine

*George's Marvelous Medicine,* like *Danny, the Champion of the World,* grew out of an earlier Dahl story. The basic plot that Dahl used in *George's Marvelous Medicine* came from the second half of *Charlie and the Great Glass Elevator.* In both stories Dahl wrote about a cranky old woman who takes a dose of mysterious medicine and then experiences a series of changes. In *George's Marvelous Medicine,* however, Dahl more fully developed this plot line. He also made the story into more of an aggression fantasy. In 1981 the London publisher Jonathan Cape brought out the book, with illustrations by Quentin Blake.

The two major characters in *George's Marvelous Medicine* are George, an eight-year-old boy, and his cantankerous grandmother, who is simply called Grandma. George is portrayed as a normal boy, but Grandma resembles a witch. She is physically repulsive. In addition to being shriveled up, she has "pale brown teeth and a small puckered-up mouth like a dog's bottom."[7] Her behavior, however, is worse than her looks. She is described as "always complaining, grousing, grouching, grumbling, griping about something or other. . . . She didn't seem to care about other people, only herself. She was a miserable old grouch" (*George,* 2). Grandma is especially mean to her grandson, always ordering him about, criticizing his every move, calling him names, and worst of all, trying to make him eat various insects.

The plot hinges on George's decision to get even with Grandma. He creates a ghastly concoction of cleaning products, foodstuffs, automobile fluids, and practically everything else that he finds around the house and pours a little bit of it into the jar containing Grandma's medicine. When Grandma takes a spoonful of George's brew she undergoes a whole array of ridiculous transformations.

She keeps consuming George's medicine, even when he tells her not to, and this finally brings about her amazing demise. Although George's aggression clearly fuels the story, it is dealt with in such a humorous and whimsical manner that it hardly seems as if he is out to murder his grandmother. Rather, it seems more as if George is simply playing a prank on her. Grandma is the one who comes across as being ultimately responsible for causing the prank to get out of hand.

Soon after its publication *George's Marvelous Medicine* began to attract controversy. While some reviewers, such as Nicholas Tucker, enjoyed the book's humor,[8] a number of other reviewers and critics vehemently attacked the book. The reviewer for the *Economist,* for example, said that "Dahl seems actually to advocate murdering the more irritating members of the family and to make it acceptable."[9] Similarily, David Rees, a prominent critic in the field of children's literature, argued that the book teaches children that grumpy people "deserve to be poisoned and killed."[10]

Dahl dismissed as ludicrous the charge that his book teaches children to murder their relatives. Children, he argued, would never interpret the book in such a literal fashion. As he put it, "Children know that the violence in my stories is only make-believe. It's much like the violence in the old fairy tales. . . . These tales are pretty rough, but the violence is confined to a magical time and place. When violence is tied to fantasy and humor, children find it . . . amusing" (West 1988, 75). Dahl's position found support in a study conducted by Charles Gerard Van Renen. As part of his study Van Renen surveyed a group of schoolchildren about their reactions to *George's Marvelous Medicine,* and he discovered that "few respondents were prepared to take the situation seriously" and that nearly all felt "that the events of this fantasy would find no ready transfer to real life."[11]

## The BFG

Dahl's tendency to use one story as a springboard for another is evident when one examines the history of *The BFG.* The origins of this book can be found in the second chapter of *Danny, the*

*Champion of the World.* In that chapter Danny's father tells his son a series of bedtime stories "about an enormous fellow called 'The Big Friendly Giant,' or 'The BFG' for short" (*Danny,* 9). As the father tells it, the BFG lives in an underground cavern, where he has a powder factory. Every night he ventures out of his cavern and blows a bit of his magical powder on sleeping children, which causes them to have wonderful dreams. Dahl used this chapter to develop the father's personality and to give a sense of the relationship between the father and Danny. He put some of the elements of the chapter to another use in his 1982 book *The BFG.* Illustrated by Quentin Blake, *The BFG* was published in England by Jonathan Cape and in America by Farrar, Straus & Giroux. Of all the children's books that he had written up to that point, Dahl saw *The BFG* as his best (Powling, 70).

As portrayed in the book, the BFG retains many of the characteristics he has in *Danny, the Champion of the World.* In both books he is a likeable giant who lives in a cave and devotes his life to collecting and administering dreams. Also, in both books, the BFG has very sensitive hearing, which enables him to detect the sounds of dreams buzzing through the air. The only real difference between the two portrayals is that in *Danny* the BFG runs a powder factory and uses his powders to administer dreams, whereas in *The BFG* he neither makes nor uses any type of powder.

Although most of the surface characteristics of the BFG are sketched out in *Danny,* in *The BFG* he becomes a real character with an interesting background and a distinct personality. He is part of a community of 10 giants, all of whom live in Giant Country, a remote part of the world that humans have not discovered. The other giants are much larger and meaner than the BFG. They regularly eat children, but the BFG disapproves of this behavior. Instead, he eats a foul-tasting vegetable called the snozzcumber, which is the only type of food that grows in Giant Country. He is by far the most intelligent of the giants, but he is entirely self-educated. As a result he often mixes up words and ignores grammatical rules. For example, when describing the taste of snozzcumbers, he says, "I squoggle it! I mispise it! I dispunge it! But because I is refusing to gobble up human beans like the other giants, I must spend my life guzzling up icky-poo snozzcumbers instead. If I don't, I will be nothing but skin and groans."[12] There is, in other words, a touch of nonsense poetry in everything he says.

The other major character in *The BFG* is Sophie. She is about eight or nine years old and lives in a village orphanage somewhere in England. With her thick glasses, Sophie appears to be quiet and bookish, but she is actually a spunky girl who is not easily intimidated. Her natural inquisitiveness leads her to spot the BFG when he is on one of his nightly rounds. This results in her being captured by the BFG and taken to Giant Country. She learns that he means her no harm, but he cannot release her because he fears that she will tell other humans about his existence. Initially, she is a bit frightened by the BFG, but she never panics. Sophie soon begins to like the BFG, and she readily sides with him in his feud with the other giants.

Sophie and the BFG become coconspirators in a daring plan to stop the other giants from eating children. This plan provides the book with its basic plot. All of the book's other elements, such as the BFG's dream business and the growing friendship between Sophie and the BFG, feed into this story line. Thus, even though there are many different facets to the book, the story does not seem episodic. Another noteworthy feature of the plot is that it is driven by decisions made mostly by Sophie. Unlike Charlie Bucket, Sophie is not simply a passive observer. She makes plans, takes risks, and exercises leadership. Because she plays such an active role in the story, the spinning of the plot contributes to her character development and vice versa.

Like most of Dahl's children's books, *The BFG* is filled with humor, much of which is tied to wordplay. This type of humor abounds in the statements made by the BFG; every time he opens his mouth he utters strings of puns and silly-sounding words. Also, like Dahl's other children's books, *The BFG* contains many humorous scenes in which powerful or authoritarian figures are ridiculed. In one scene, for example, the mean giants become the

butt of an elaborate prank played by the BFG. In another scene
the heads of the army and the air force are made to appear very
foolish.

The *BFG* does contain one form of humor that is not generally
found in Dahl's other children's books. This humor deals with bodily functions and the reactions that people often have to them.
Toward the beginning of the book the BFG introduces Sophie to a
fizzy beverage called frobscottle. Once consumed, frobscottle
causes flatulence. The BFG refers to this side effect as whizzpopping, and he is not at all embarrassed about it. As he explains to
the astonished Sophie, "Us giants is making whizzpoppers all the
time! Whizzpopping is a sign of happiness. It is music to our ears!
You surely is not telling me that a little whizzpopping is forbidden
among human beans" (*BFG,* 65).

The scenes related to whizzpopping, though they are among the
funniest in the book, break the taboo against mentioning bodily
functions in children's literature. Dahl was well aware of this
long-standing taboo, but he decided to ignore it. When asked how
he came to this decision, he said, "Children regard bodily functions as being both mysterious and funny, and that's why they
often joke about these things. Bodily functions also serve to hu-
manize adults. There is nothing that makes a child laugh more
than an adult suddenly farting in a room. If it were a queen, it
would be even funnier. I try to capture this type of humor in *The
BFG,* but instead of calling it farting, I call it whizzpopping. . . . I
put it in because it makes me, with my childish mind, laugh, and
I know it makes children laugh" (West 1988, 75–76).

In the case of *The BFG* Dahl's taboo breaking did not concern
most of the people who reviewed the book. Almost without exception the reviewers praised the humor in the book. Judith Elkin, a
reviewer for the *Times Literary Supplement,* called *The BFG* "the
funniest and the most appealing book that [Dahl] has written for
a long time." She went on to say that the book's "nonsensical wordplay and deliciously witty use of language will undoubtedly appeal to the child's crude sense of fun and delight in jokey
phrases."[13] In a review published in the *Spectator* Gillian Avery
wrote, "[*The BFG*] is very funny and exciting, and moves at a

crackling pace. There are also some satisfyingly rude jokes."[14] Ruth I. Gordon, who reviewed the book for the *New York Times Book Review,* predicted that some adults would be " offended" by some of the book's humorous passages, but she threw her support behind the book. *"The BFG* is a success," she wrote, "since it allows children a recognition of the habits, dreams and humor that they alone possess. Dahl appeals to a child's sense of justice, morbidity and humor. An occasional humorous finger poked at the established habits of the world should harm no one and delight many."[15]

## The Witches

*The Witches* made its debut in 1983, just a year after the publication of *The BFG.* The two books are similar in several ways. In each case, Jonathan Cape brought out the first English edition, and shortly thereafter Farrar, Straus & Giroux brought out an American edition. Also, Quentin Blake illustrated both books. More important than these surface commonalities, however, are the similarities in the stories' plots and characters. Each book uses as its backdrop a conflict between children and one of children's traditional enemies from fairy tales. The protagonist in each story is an orphan who sets out to save the children of the world from their supernatural foe. Also, in each book the orphan has an elderly ally who, in addition to helping the young hero defeat the enemy, is a source of much-needed emotional support. Despite these similarities the books are somewhat different in tone. *The Witches* is more suspenseful and a bit more serious than *The BFG.*

The central character in *The Witches* is a seven-year-old boy. This character, whose name is never revealed, also serves as the story's narrator. He is from England, but he often visits Norway, where his grandmother lives. On one of these visits his parents are killed in an automobile accident, and he is left in the custody of his grandmother. He and his grandmother move back to England so that he can continue to live in his old home and attend his regular school. For the most part his life returns to normal, but his eccentric grandmother makes sure that his life never becomes so normal that it seems dull.

The grandmother is 86, but she is still quite sprightly and playful. She smokes smelly cigars, tells exciting stories, and agrees with her grandson that children should not bathe too frequently. Her most unusual attribute, however, is that she is a retired witchophile. When her grandson asks her what this means, she explains that a witchophile is "a person who studies witches, and knows a lot about them."[16] He is curious about witches, so she tells him how witches operate and how to distinguish them from ordinary women.

The grandmother's depiction of witches is much more detailed than the descriptions found in most fairy tales. As she describes them, witches have bald heads, clawed fingers, toeless feet, large nostrils, and blue saliva, but they take great pains to hide these features when they are in the presence of nonwitches. According to the grandmother, the witches in one country have little contact with witches from other countries, but they all answer to the Grand High Witch. The goal of all these witches is to rid the world of children, and they try to accomplish this by transforming children into slugs and other creatures. The information that the grandmother provides about witches serves as an introduction to the book's central plot.

The heart of the book deals with a series of events that occur while the boy and his grandmother are vacationing in the seaside town of Bournmouth. They are staying at the Hotel Magnificent, which happens to be where the witches of England are holding their annual convention. The boy overhears the witches discussing a plan to turn all of the children in England into mice. While he is eavesdropping the witches detect his presence and turn him into a mouse. The hero finds that he actually likes being a mouse, and the grandmother has no objections to having a mouse for a grandson. Nevertheless, the two agree that the witches must be prevented from implementing their plan. For the rest of the story the hero and his grandmother wage a secret, and ultimately successful, campaign against the witches.

Although there are many humorous scenes in *The Witches,* the book is not as lighthearted as *The BFG.* One of the reasons for this is that the boy in *The Witches* experiences the death of his parents during the course of the story, whereas Sophie has never really known her parents. Also, the villains in *The Witches* seem a bit more sinister than the comical giants in *The BFG.* That the witches are disguised as ordinary people gives them an ominous quality lacking in the giants. Perhaps the most important reason *The Witches* seems more serious than *The BFG* has to do with the books' conclusions. Unlike Sophie, the hero of *The Witches* does not escape unscathed from his encounters with the villains of the story. Not only does he have to spend the rest of his life as a mouse; his life span is shortened considerably, because mice do not live nearly as long as people do. Although the reader may feel sad that the hero's problems are not dismissed with the wave of a magic wand, this does not mean that the book has a sad ending. Both the hero and his grandmother accept the changes in their lives and are eager to set out on new adventures. Nevertheless, when compared with *The BFG*'s fairy-tale ending, the conclusion to *The Witches* seems somewhat truer to real life.

*The Witches* generated some controversy among reviewers and critics. Several called the book sexist because many of the females in the book come across as being evil.[17] In making their charges these detractors often cited the following passage from the beginning of the book: "A witch is always a woman. I do not wish to speak badly about women. Most women are lovely. But the fact remains that all witches are women" (*Witches,* 6). David Rees, one of the people who considered the book to be sexist, interpreted this passage in a literal way. Adopting the tone of a lawyer rebutting erroneous court testimony, Rees carefully pointed out that some men were charged with practicing witchcraft during the famous witch trials in Salem, Massachusetts (Rees, 147). The charges of sexism actually led to the banning of *The Witches* from some libraries in England.[18]

In America the book was not censored, but it did attract the ire of one unusual group. Dahl received a number of angry letters from American women who belonged to societies of witches and felt that he had given a false impression of witches. One letter writer, for example, told Dahl, "This book must be taken off the shelves. We are not such bad people" (West 1988, 73).

Although some people spoke out against *The Witches,* many others championed the book. It won the prestigious Whitbread Award, and both the American Library Association and the *New York Times* designated it as one of the best children's books of the year. The book also attracted the attention of Jim Henson, the famous puppeteer, who used it as the basis for the last film that he produced. Released in 1990, the film stars Anjelica Huston as the Grand High Witch, Mai Zetterling as the grandmother, and Jasen Fisher as the young hero.

Support for the book also came from numerous book reviewers, including *Newsweek's* Walter Clemons, who especially liked the grandmother,[19] and *Horn Book's* Nancy C. Hammond, who described the story as "an appealing, fanciful tale of devotion."[20] Perhaps the most thoughtful review came from Erica Jong. Writing for the *New York Times Book Review,* Jong argued that Dahl's witches should not be compared to the real women who have been labeled witches. "His witches," she wrote, "must be horrifying creatures to underline the hero's heroism." Jong went on to praise Dahl for writing a story that is both exciting and emotionally moving. She concluded by commenting on the relationship between the two major characters: "*The Witches* is finally a love story—the story of a little boy who loves his grandmother so utterly (and she him) that they are looking forward to spending their last years . . . exterminating the witches of the world together. It is a curious sort of tale but an honest one, which deals with matters of crucial importance to children: smallness, the existence of evil in the world, mourning, separation, death."[21]

As Jong's review suggests, Dahl's depiction of the grandmother belies the charge that the book presents women in a sexist light. Not only is the grandmother portrayed as a loving and understanding woman, but she also possesses qualities often associated with male heroes. She is wise, brave, and totally unflappable. Thus, even though the witches in the book come across as villainous, this negative image of females is counterbalanced by the positive image provided by the grandmother.

## *Matilda*

*Matilda* came out in April 1988. Like Dahl's other children's books from the 1980s, it was illustrated by Quentin Blake and published by Jonathan Cape. In no time *Matilda* became one of Cape's bestsellers. Toward the end of the same year Viking Kestrel brought out the first American edition, and it too met with tremendous success. The book quickly became a hit in other countries as well. It achieved best-seller status in France, West Germany, Italy, Spain, and especially Holland. In the span of less than two years, over 120,000 hardcover copies of the book were sold in Holland alone. Even Dahl, who had become accustomed to high sales figures, called the figures from Holland startling.

Compared with most of Dahl's children's books, *Matilda* is more closely tied to the real world. It features no fantasy creatures such as Oompa-Loompas or witches. It is set in modern-day England, and none of the characters visit magical factories or unknown countries where giants roam. The fantasy element of telekinesis does play a pivotal role in the final part of the story, but most of the other unusual occurences in the book are products of exaggeration. In its reliance on exaggeration over outright fantasy, *Matilda* is more similar to *Danny, the Champion of the World* than any of Dahl's other books for young readers.

Matilda, like Sophie from *The BFG,* is an independent girl who is curious about life and not easily intimidated by powerful adults. In addition, however, Matilda is a child prodigy. She had taught herself to read at the age of three, and by the time she was five she had already read many full-length adult novels, including the complete works of Charles Dickens. Another sign of her phenomenal intelligence is that she can easily work out complex mathematical problems in her head. Although she is clearly a genius, she is not at all conceited. One of the reasons for this is that her parents are oblivious to her special gifts. It is not until she enters school that she realizes that her abilities are unusual.

Matilda's parents, Mr. and Mrs. Wormwood, are portrayed as despicable people. They are arrogant, unethical, and totally uninterested in any intellectual pursuits other than those associated with making money. Mr. Wormwood owns a used-car lot, and he prides himself on thinking of new ways to cheat his customers. Mrs. Wormwood spends most of her time watching television and playing bingo. Although they seem to care for each other, neither parent has any interest in Matilda. Most of the time they ignore her. When they do talk to her it is usually to criticize her for reading too much or to accuse her of lying. They are a bit more loving toward their son, who is several years older than Matilda, but they do not spend much time with him either.

Even worse than Mr. and Mrs. Wormwood is Miss Trunchbull, the headmistress of Matilda's school. The Wormwoods are guilty of child neglect, but Miss Trunchbull regularly commits child abuse. A former Olympic hammer thrower, Miss Trunchbull uses her special throwing skills to hurl children through windows. Like a stereotypical drill sergeant, Miss Trunchbull constantly barks orders, suppresses individuality, and ruthlessly punishes anyone who questions her judgment or authority. The law prohibits her from caning the students, but she still finds many ways to punish them. Aside from flinging students out the window, her favorite form of punishment is to lock the students up for several hours in a narrow cupboard lined with broken glass and metal spikes.

The only kind adult in the story is Matilda's teacher, a young woman named Miss Honey. She is described as "a mild and quiet person who never raised her voice and was seldom seen to smile, but there is no doubt she possessed that rare gift for being adored by every small child under her care."[22] Miss Honey immediately realizes that Matilda is much more advanced than the other students in the class, and she does everything she can to provide Matilda with appropriate curricular materials. As the story progresses Miss Honey and Matilda develop a close and mutually rewarding relationship.

At its core *Matilda* is a story about the struggle against tyranny.

The early chapters focus on Matilda's responses to her parents' oppressive behavior. In her dealings with her parents she refuses to play the role of the helpless victim. Each time her parents treat her in a cruel or demeaning manner, she retaliates by playing a clever prank on one or both of them. After she enters school the primary target of her plotting is Miss Trunchbull. Matilda has some unpleasant encounters with Miss Trunchbull, but this is not the only reason she despises the headmistress. Matilda is also repelled by the way Miss Trunchbull brutalizes the other students and intimidates Miss Honey. Thus, when Matilda decides to take on Miss Trunchbull she is motivated by much more than personal revenge. She hopes to strike a blow in behalf of all the people who have suffered under Miss Trunchbull's tyranny.

Although Matilda proves to be the most effective resistance fighter in the campaign against Miss Trunchbull, other characters also take part in it. A number of students defy Miss Trunchbull in small but amusing ways. One girl, for example, puts an itching powder in Miss Trunchbull's shorts, and another girl puts a newt in her pitcher of drinking water. These pranks do not seriously undermine Miss Trunchbull's power, but they cause her some embarrassment.

Miss Honey also tries to resist the headmistress, but this takes all the courage she can muster. Toward the end of the book it is revealed that she has good cause to be extremely frightened by Miss Trunchbull, for she spent much of her childhood living with the tyrant. As Miss Honey tells Matilda, she is Miss Trunchbull's niece, and she was left in her aunt's custody after the death of her parents. In recalling this difficult period in her life, Miss Honey says, "I became so completely cowed and dominated by this monster of an aunt that when she gave me an order, no matter what it was, I obeyed it instantly" (*Matilda*, 199).

Now that she is an adult, Miss Honey is still afraid to disobey her aunt, even though she believes that her aunt does not deserve to be obeyed. Miss Honey partially attributes her reluctance to stand up to her aunt to the fact that she has a "shy and retiring" personality. In her efforts to change this aspect of her personality, she looks to Matilda as her role model. Because of her own unhappy childhood, Miss Honey knows that Matilda's difficult home situation could easily erode her sense of self-worth, but Matilda does not allow this to happen. It is this inner strength that Miss Honey admires and wishes to emulate.

Matilda's inner strength serves as an inspiration not only to Miss Honey but to the reader as well. There is a heroic quality to Matilda's character that is even more impressive than her incredible intelligence. Like Meg Murry from Madeleine L'Engle's *A Wrinkle in Time,* Matilda has some remarkable talents, but it is her indomitable spirit that makes her a hero.

Matilda's character appealed to many of the people who reviewed the book, including Vicki Weissman, a writer for the *New York Times Book Review.* She began her review by emphatically stating, "I like Matilda." Weissman went on to say that she admired Matilda's intelligence and independence and liked the fact that "Matilda knows how to be extremely and creatively naughty."[23] Linda Taylor, who reviewed the book for the *Times Literary Supplement,* called Matilda a "good addition to the Dahl oeuvre." Taylor especially enjoyed the way Matilda "defeats . . . nasty adults." Both Weissman and Taylor pointed out that Matilda has much in common with the child characters from Dahl's other books. As Taylor put it, all these "children are given inventive powers to bounce back and revenge themselves humorously against their oppressors."[24]

While it is true that Matilda and the other young heroes from Dahl's books are similar in certain ways, they are not exact copies of each other. Their differences become readily apparent when one looks at these characters in their order of appearance. James and Charlie, the heroes from Dahl's first major children's books, are quiet and well-behaved boys who take a fairly passive approach to life. They need the help of mysterious benefactors in order to improve their unhappy living conditions. Danny is also a polite child, but he shows more initiative than do James or Charlie. Still, he is quite dependent on his father. He counts on his father not only to provide the necessities of life but also to entertain him. George is much more independent than his three predecessors. He entertains himself and tries to solve his own problems. However, he tends not to concern himself about anybody's troubles but his own. Sophie and the boy from *The Witches* share George's independence, but they are less self-centered than George. Both of these characters put themselves in dangerous situations in order to help other children. Although these two characters are resourceful and brave, they cannot accomplish their missions without the help of older characters.

Compared to Dahl's other child characters, Matilda is the most independent as well as the most capable of solving problems. Not only is she undaunted by adults, but she seldom needs adult assistance. Like Sophie and the boy from *The Witches,* Matilda cares about the problems of other people. Indeed, she is one of the few child characters from Dahl's books to care enough about an adult's problems to try to do something about them. Thus, even though Matilda has many points in common with the characters who came before her, she stands out as the noblest of them all.

# 6

# Writing for the Nippers

When Dahl spoke informally he sometimes referred to young children—those between the ages of around three and seven—as nippers. He enjoyed interacting with children from this age group, but he generally wrote for a somewhat older audience. He did, however, experiment with writing stories for younger children, and the experience convinced him that this is a difficult age to reach. He elaborated on this point during an interview:

> All good children's books take a lot of effort, but I find it hardest to write books for the very young, books to be read by the mother or father while the child is in bed. . . . Most of the books for this age are written by illustrators. They can usually draw the pictures, but many of them can't write. This goes back to Beatrix Potter. I asked a children's book publisher what she would do if she received three or four of Potter's manuscripts without any of her illustrations, and the publisher said she would send them back. Now, if you put the pictures with it, it's another matter. My point is that it is very difficult to come up with a plot that will hold a four-year-old's attention without the aid of illustrations. (West 1990, 64)

Over the years Dahl published seven stories for younger children: *The Magic Finger* (1966), *Fantastic Mr. Fox* (1970), *The Enormous Crocodile* (1977), *The Twits* (1980), *The Giraffe and the Pelly and Me* (1985), *Esio Trot* (1990), and *The Minpins* (published posthumously in 1991). With the exception of *Esio Trot,* these books are fantasy stories. Unlike most of Dahl's fantasy stories for older children, his books for younger children usually contain anthropomorphic animals. Another difference between these two groups of books is that there tends to be a greater emphasis on imparting a moral message in his books for younger children.

## *The Magic Finger*

*The Magic Finger* began as Dahl's contribution to a proposed anthology of children's stories by prominent writers for adults. Crowell-Collier, the publisher of the planned anthology, required that the contributors use only words that a beginning reader could readily understand. Dahl reluctantly adhered to this requirement, but it bothered him because he felt that it produced stilted language and deprived children of opportunities to learn new words. Soon after finishing this story he vowed never to write another restricted-word story and said that he was "very sorry" he had ever done so ("Let's Build," 2).

After some of the other contributors sent in their stories, Crowell-Collier lost interest in the project. Apparently, the publisher liked Dahl's story but was disappointed in most of the other contributions (Powling, 67). Dahl eventually decided to see if someone else would be interested in publishing the story in the form of a picture book. Harper & Row bought the manuscript and arranged to have William Pène du Bois supply black-and-white illustrations. The book came out in America in 1966, and two years later Allen & Unwin published a British edition.

The magic finger mentioned in the title belongs to a young girl who also serves as the narrator of the story. When she is angry the tip of her forefinger becomes tingly. If she then points her finger at the person who has provoked her, strange events take place. The story focuses on such an occasion. One Saturday morning she attempts to convince her neighbors, a family called the Greggses, to stop shooting deer and ducks. They brush her aside and tell her to mind her own business. Their brusque response makes her mad and prompts her to "put the magic finger on them all!"[1] That evening the Greggses shrink to the size of ducks and grow duck wings in place of their arms. When they realize what has happened they decide to leave their house and try out their new wings. While they are out flying a family of huge ducks who have arms instead of wings move into the Greggses' house. The next morning the ducks take the Greggses' guns and go hunting. The Greggses discover that when the roles are reversed, they no longer find hunting to be such an enjoyable activity.

The story clearly conveys the message that hunting is a cruel sport. It also, however, makes a point about the differences between what is legal and what is moral. Toward the end of the story the Greggses beg the huge ducks not to shoot at them. One of the ducks replies by asking, "Why not? . . . You are always shooting at us." To which Mr. Greggs says, "Oh, but that's not the same! . . . We are allowed to shoot ducks!" When the duck asks the Greggses who gave them permission to shoot ducks, Mr. Greggs answers, "We allow each other." In response to this comment, the duck says, "Very nice. . . . And now we are going to allow each other to shoot you" (*Magic,* 24). Through such scenes, the story suggests that some societal rules are designed to serve the interests of the powerful rather than the interests of justice.

When the book came out it did not attract nearly as much attention as *James and the Giant Peach* or *Charlie and the Chocolate Factory* did when they were first published. Nevertheless, the book received a number of positive reviews, including a fairly lengthy one by Alice Dalgliesh. Writing for the *Saturday Review,* Dalgliesh said that although she disliked Dahl's earlier children's books, she found this one thought-provoking and memorable. She saw the book as a timely parable and suggested that parents use it as a springboard for discussions about violence and other social and moral issues.[2]

Ironically, Dahl had some misgivings about the very aspects of the book that Dalgliesh liked. He preferred not to be known as a writer of moralistic parables. As he explained during an interview, he did not become a children's author so that he could deliver sermons. "My only purpose in writing books for children," he said, "is to encourage them to develop a love of books. I'm not trying to indoctrinate them in any way. I'm trying to entertain them" (West 1988, 73–74).

## *Fantastic Mr. Fox*

When Dahl set out to write *Fantastic Mr. Fox,* his next book for younger children, he paid particular attention to creating a fast-moving and entertaining plot. After finishing the story, he felt more satisfied with it than he had ever felt about *The Magic Finger.* He sent the manuscript to Knopf, who published it in 1970 along with ink-wash illustrations by Donald Chaffin. That same year Allen & Unwin released the book in England.

*Fantastic Mr. Fox,* like *The Magic Finger,* revolves around a conflict between humans and animals. In this case the humans are represented by three nasty farmers named Boggis, Bunce, and Bean. In addition to being mean, these farmers are physically repulsive. Bean, for example, is so filthy that "his ear holes [are] clogged with all kinds of muck and wax and bits of chewing gum and dead flies."[3] Boggis, Bunce, and Bean do battle with a family of foxes. The farmers want to kill Mr. Fox because he regularly uses their poultry to feed his family. The farmers find the entrance to the hole where the foxes live and attempt to shoot Mr. Fox when he leaves the hole. When this plan fails they decide to dig the foxes out. The foxes, however, simply dig in deeper. Finally, the farmers lay siege to the fox hole in the hope of starving the foxes to death. Mr. Fox eventually solves this problem by digging tunnels underneath the buildings in which the poultry are kept, thus making it possible for him to feed his family without going near the entrance to the fox hole.

The action-oriented plot is made even more dramatic by the characters' strong emotional reactions to the events in the story.

Each time the foxes get away, the farmers react by becoming "more furious and more obstinate and more determined than ever not to give up" (*Fox*, 21). Though the farmers seem fairly comical in the beginning of the story, their increasing fanaticism transforms them into formidable villains. On the other hand, there is a sense of pathos to the foxes' reactions to the campaign against them. Their physical and emotional sufferings are convincingly described, and this helps the reader care about their plight. Also, the reader cannot help but admire the foxes' bravery and their unflagging devotion to each other. The story, in other words, is not only exciting; it is also emotionally engaging.

Another interesting feature of the story is its subterranean setting. Several of Dahl's earlier books, including *The Gremlins* and *Charlie and the Chocolate Factory,* also feature underground settings. In these earlier books characters move below ground in order to protect their secrets. In *Fantastic Mr. Fox,* however, the underground setting is used to convey a sense of community among a group of characters. The animals who live underground—the foxes, badgers, moles, weasels, and rabbits—all see themselves as "diggers." They fear the open ground and spend as much time as they can in their burrows and tunnels. Their shared love of the underground bonds them together and causes them to care about each other's welfare.

Although the plot to *Fantastic Mr. Fox* is not built around a moral lesson, the story does have some intriguing moral implications. This aspect of the book is most evident when Badger, one of the secondary characters, asks Mr. Fox if he feels guilty about stealing the farmers' poultry. In response to this question, Mr. Fox says that he is not trying to harm the farmers, even though the farmers are trying to kill him. He is just doing what he needs to do in order to keep his family alive. As he puts it to Badger, "Do you know anyone in the whole world who wouldn't swipe a few chickens if their children were starving to death?" (*Fox*, 45). Mr. Fox clearly places a greater value on protecting his family than on respecting private property. Thus, the story contains at least a suggestion that there is more to morality than obeying societal rules.

A few reviewers made mention of the book's unconventional morality, but this did not stop them from recommending the story. Margaret Fisher, for example, described the book as being "cheerfully amoral," but she also called it a "robust tale" and described Mr. Fox as a "worthy descendant of the medieval Renard."[4] Indeed, practically everyone who reviewed *Fantastic Mr. Fox* seemed to like it. Many reviewers, including Ingeborg Boudreau of the *New York Times Book Review,* praised the fast-paced plot. "It's an edge-of-your-seat kind of story," Boudreau wrote, "with a makes-you-feel-good-all-over ending."[5] A reviewer for *Publishers Weekly* went so far as to hail the book's publication as "cause for rejoicing."[6]

## The Enormous Crocodile

Although Dahl saw *The Magic Finger* and *Fantastic Mr. Fox* as suitable for preschool-age children, he aimed these books primarily at children in the beginning grades of school. *The Enormous Crocodile,* however, was written specifically for preschoolers. Given the book's intended audience, Dahl and his new English publisher, Jonathan Cape, were especially concerned about finding the right illustrator. Luckily, Quentin Blake, one of England's foremost illustrators, agreed to provide full-color illustrations for the book, thus marking the start of a long series of collaborations with Dahl. In the fall of 1978 Cape published *The Enormous Crocodile,* complete with Blake's humorous illustrations, and around Christmas Knopf brought out the first American edition.

The story takes place in Africa and features several African animals as characters. In addition to the Enormous Crocodile, there is Humpy-Rumpy the Hippopotamus, Trunky the Elephant, Muggle-Wump the Monkey, and Roly-Poly Bird. Except for the crocodile, these animals are friendly and get along well with the people who live in the nearby town. The Enormous Crocodile, however, is not at all friendly. He is a boastful, greedy, and maniacal creature who constantly mistreats the other animals. Worst of all, he has a penchant for eating the children from the town.

At the beginning of the story, the Enormous Crocodile announces his intention to sneak into town and eat several children for lunch. Another crocodile reminds him that the last time he tried to sneak into town all the children saw him coming and ran in the other direction, but the Enormous Crocodile insists that this time it will be different. When asked why, he says, "Nobody will see me because this time I've thought up secret plans and clever tricks."[7]

For the rest of the story the Enormous Crocodile tries various disguises in order to fool the children into coming close enough for him to gobble them up, but each time he is about to sink his teeth into "a nice juicy little child" (*Crocodile*), one of the other animals comes along and foils his plan. Once, for example, he disguises himself as a coconut tree. Some children spot the coconuts that he is holding and are about to go after them when the hippopotamus charges out of the jungle and smacks into the Enormous Crocodile, sending him "tumbling and skidding over the ground" (*Crocodile*). In the end the elephant comes up with a unique way of making sure that the Enormous Crocodile will never cause any more trouble.

In terms of its plot, central character, and moral message, the story has much in common with traditional fairy tales. Like "The Three Little Pigs" and numerous other fairy tales, *The Enormous Crocodile* establishes a pattern early in the story and then repeats it, with slight variations, until the final scene. The story's villain is similar to the wolves in both "The Three Little Pigs" and "Little Red Riding Hood." All these villainous characters try to deceive young innocents in order to make meals of them, but they are eventually defeated despite their great strength and craftiness. In a sense all these stories give the impression that the world is not a safe place for the young and the weak, but they also imply that even the most powerful villains are not invincible.

The book received mostly favorable reviews. A number of reviewers predicted that young children would find the plot very appealing. For example, Elaine Moss of the *Times Literary Supplement* said that "the story will be asked for again and again because the vicarious thrill of *almost* being eaten by a crocodile is infinitely desirable."[8] Similarly, Elizabeth Jane Howard of the *New Statesman* said that Dahl "understands the symmetry of story-telling that young children do like—a kind of near predictability saved from being boring by good, ingenious invention."[9] Several other reviewers, including Georgess McHargue of the *New York Times Book Review,* praised the language in the story. As McHargue stated in her review, "Dahl's gift for sonorous and inventive language carries the story along merrily."[10] Practically all the reviewers greatly admired Blake's illustrations. Virginia Haviland of the *Horn Book* echoed the sentiments of her fellow reviewers when she called Blake "a perfect choice to illustrate the . . . tale."[11]

Blake's ability to capture the spirit of Dahl's story is tied in some ways to the relationship that the two men formed while working on this book. Rather than simply illustrate Dahl's story, Blake entered into a collaboration with Dahl. Blake and Dahl talked at length about the pictures, and Blake often changed the pictures as a result of these discussions.

## The Twits

With *The Twits* Dahl returned to writing for children in the beginning grades of school. He wrote the story at about the same length and reading level as *Fantastic Mr. Fox.* Once Dahl finished writing *The Twits* it was given to Quentin Blake to illustrate. Jonathan Cape brought out the book in England in 1980, and the next year Knopf published it in America.

The central characters in *The Twits* are an elderly couple known simply as Mr. and Mrs. Twit. Like the farmers in *Fantastic Mr. Fox,* Mr. and Mrs. Twit are both morally and physically repulsive. Before retiring, the Twits had worked as animal trainers for a circus and had regularly abused the animals under their care. They still have a family of four monkeys, and Mr. Twit, who dreams of starting an upside-down monkey circus, forces the monkeys to spend six hours every day standing on their heads. The Twits are even more abusive to the area birds. Each week they slaughter dozens of birds and bake them in a bird pie. The Twits are just as ugly as they are cruel. Mr. Twit has a big, bristly beard that he never trims or cleans. As a result, it is full of all sorts of disgusting things, such as "a piece of maggoty green cheese or a moldy old corn flake or even the slimy tail of a tinned sardine."[12] Although Mrs. Twit does not have a filthy beard, she is not much more attractive than her husband. She is constantly frowning, and her hair is nearly as unkempt as Mr. Twit's beard.

Mr. and Mrs. Twit are similar not only to the farmers from *Fantastic Mr. Fox* but also to the Enormous Crocodile. The Twits share the crocodile's love of playing nasty tricks on people. For the most part, however, the Twits torment each other with their tricks. On one occasion Mrs. Twit puts her glass eye in Mr. Twit's beer mug, and he nearly swallows it. Another time she pours spaghetti sauce over a plateful of live worms and serves it to her unsuspecting husband. Mr. Twit is just as bad. He, for example, sticks a slimy frog in Mrs. Twit's bed and then fools her into thinking that the frog is a dangerous monster.

There are also some direct connections between the most important secondary characters in *The Twits* and two characters from *The Enormous Crocodile*. Muggle-Wump, the monkey introduced in *The Enormous Crocodile,* is the father in the monkey family that the Twits own. As is briefly explained in the story, the Twits had arranged for Muggle-Wump and his family to be captured in Africa and brought to England. Roly-Poly Bird also makes an appearance in *The Twits*. Roly-Poly Bird still lives in Africa, but he flies through England during his holiday and happens to land on the monkeys' cage. Both Muggle-Wump and Roly-Poly Bird play pivotal roles in the book's conclusion.

Connections between *The Twits* and Dahl's earlier stories are especially evident in the final scenes of the book. In this case, though, the connection is with one of Dahl's most obscure stories, a one-page vignette published in the November 1945 issue of *Atlantic Monthly.* Entitled "Smoked Cheese," this little story is about a man who discovers an unusual way to get rid of the mice in his house. He turns all the furniture upside down and glues it to the ceiling. When the mice see what the man has done they decide that they are upside down. They therefore stand on their heads until they all die "from a rush of blood to the head."[13] This plot line serves as the basis for the conclusion to *The Twits.* However, the monkeys and the birds, working together under the direction of Muggle-Wump, are the ones who glue the furniture to the ceiling, and the Twits are the ones who fall for the trick and end up standing on their heads.

As is generally the case with Dahl's children's books, *The Twits* is a humorous book, but the humor is a bit cruder than that found in most of his other books. The type of humor in *The Twits* generally appeals more strongly to children than it does to adults. While some adults might be repulsed by Dahl's descriptions of Mr. and Mrs. Twit's disgusting habits and nasty pranks, most children find these passages extremely funny. One of the reasons that children like such scenes is that they are very similar to the jokes that children make about cleanliness, bodily functions, and other related topics. As Paul E. McGhee, a child psychologist and author of *Humor: Its Origin and Development,* has pointed out, scatological language and themes often figure in children's humor.[14] This helps explain why many children respond with glee when Mr. Twit is described as "a foul and smelly old man" (*Twits,* 7). In the opinions of children, Dahl's depictions of revolting behavior are made even funnier by the fact that this behavior is attributed to adults. Psychologists have long noted that children enjoy jokes and stories that poke fun at the moral authority of adults. In the words of Martha Wolfenstein, the author of *Children's Humor: A Psychological Analysis,* children "seize with delight on opportunities to show that grown-ups are not infallibly good."[15]

Predictably, the critical response to *The Twits* was sharply divided. Karla Kuskin, one of the book's detractors, was put off by the book's humor. Writing for the *New York Times Book Review,* Kuskin argued that "the humor dwells on rather elementary physical jokes, only a few of which are funny."[16] David Rees, another detractor, called *The Twits* "a disgusting book" and suggested that it would cause children "to think that all ugly people

are evil" (Rees, 146–47). Other critics, however, took a more positive view. Gillian Cross, who recommended the book in a review
published in the *Times Literary Supplement,* said that children
would enjoy reading about the Twits's repulsiveness. "Many
adults prefer to ignore this kind of crude delight in the disgusting," Cross wrote, "but most children share it at some time and all
but the very squeamish will revel in finding it recognized in *The
Twits.*"[17] Expanding on Cross's position, Charles Sarland argued
that the book's humor complements the antiauthoritarian theme
that runs throughout the story. In an article published in *Signal*
Sarland wrote:

> First, for all that the Twits are plainly set up by Dahl as
> public enemy number one, a very important element of
> their nastiness is their arbitrary exercise of authority. In
> their relationship with the monkeys and the birds, in-
> deed, it is the dominant element. And . . . the central plot
> development involves the overthrow of that arbitrary
> authority by the persecuted underdogs.
>
> Second, in a number of ways, Dahl clearly lines up with
> the child reader. . . . He mentions the unmentionable, he
> explores the limits of the *child's* world. . . . The tricks
> that the Twits play on each other are tricks that *children*
> would like to play on each other, or they are tricks that
> *children* report as having been played by friends of
> friends.
>
> In other words, in subject matter and content the book
> is plainly part of the culture of childhood. And not only
> that, it explores themes and interests that many adults
> would rather not know about. In that sense it is part of
> an oppositional culture.[18]

Sarland's idea that *The Twits* belongs to "an oppositional culture" helps explain why some adults have such vehement reactions against it. For David Rees and similarly minded adults, the
book represents a threat to the dominant, adult-controlled culture.

## *The Giraffe and the Pelly and Me*

Dahl directed *The Giraffe and the Pelly and Me* at the same preschool age audience that he had in mind when he wrote *The Enormous Crocodile*. He therefore kept the story fairly short and included lots of action. Given the book's intended audience, Quentin Blake illustrated it with numerous watercolors. Jonathan Cape published the book in England in 1985, and that same year Farrar, Straus & Giroux published it in America.

The story focuses on three animals—a giraffe, a pelican, and a monkey—who start a business called the Ladderless Window-Cleaning Company. Each animal is uniquely suited for a particular aspect of the business. Giraffe has a magical neck that can extend into the clouds, enabling her to reach the highest windows of any building. Pelican has a tremendous beak that can hold plenty of water for window washing, and Monkey has the strength and agility to stand on Giraffe's head and wash windows at the same time. Working together, they can handle even the most difficult window-washing jobs.

The story also features two important human characters: Billy, who serves as the story's narrator, and the Duke of Hampshire. Billy is a young boy who befriends the animals and goes with them on their first job. The Duke of Hampshire is the one who first hires the animals. The Duke owns a mansion with 677 windows, none of which has been cleaned for 50 years. Although the Duke initially treats Billy and the animals rather gruffly, he soon becomes their friend and benefactor.

Compared to Dahl's other stories for young children, *The Giraffe and the Pelly and Me* has a much less structured plot. The story is essentially a series of related episodes. It starts with Billy meeting the animals and learning about their window-cleaning business. The next part of the story concentrates on the Duke and his reactions to the animals. It then goes on to deal with a conflict between the animals and a burglar whom they catch stealing the Duchess's jewelry. After this incident is resolved the story focuses on how the Duke rewards the animals for catching the burglar. In the final section the Duke helps Billy start a candy store.

Another difference between *The Giraffe and the Pelly and Me* and Dahl's other children's books is that it does not break any taboos. It contains no grotesque passages and includes very little violence. Except for the burglar, all the characters are kind and reasonably well behaved. The Duke and the other adult authority figures are presented in a respectful light, and social institutions are not ridiculed. Insofar as the story has a moral message, it is a fairly conventional one about the value of cooperation.

The noncontroversial nature of the story pleased some reviewers, including the person who reviewed the book for the *Economist.* This reviewer began by deriding Dahl's other children's books but then went on to describe this one as "a witty and winning tale."[19] Similarly, the *Horn Book,* whose reviewers had disapproved of many of Dahl's earlier books, published a highly favorable review of *The Giraffe and the Pelly and Me,* calling it "a captivating story and a wonderful read-aloud."[20] Some reviewers, though, were disappointed in the book. For example, Susan Scheps, who reviewed the book for the *School Library Journal,* argued that "the minimal plot development makes this an extremely weak book."[21]

Dahl felt a bit dissatisfied with *The Giraffe and the Pelly and Me.* As he explained during an interview, he had hoped to write a book that would match the appeal of *The Enormous Crocodile.* "I tried," he said, "but I didn't quite bring it off. It's too long. It's a nice book, but it's not another *Crocodile*" (West 1990, 64). Length is one of the reasons it is not another *Crocodile,* but there are other reasons as well. While writing *The Giraffe and the Pelly and Me* Dahl ignored some of the advice that he had given to aspiring writers in an article entitled "Writing Children's Books": [a children's author] "must know what enthralls children and what bores them. They love being spooked. They love suspense. They love action. . . . They love seeing the villain meet a grisly death. . . . They like stories that contain a threat."[22]

In *The Giraffe and the Pelly and Me* Dahl provided plenty of action, but he ignored the other precepts mentioned in his article. There is nothing really spooky or suspenseful about the story. Perhaps the robber can be seen as a villain, but he is dealt with so quickly and easily that he never poses much of a threat. The same cannot be said about *The Enormous Crocodile* or most of Dahl's other books for young children. Because these books have suspenseful plots and threatening villains, they are more zestful than *The Giraffe and the Pelly and Me*.

## Esio Trot

Although *Esio Trot* was not Dahl's final book for beginning readers, it was the last one to be published while he was still alive. Jonathan Cape published the book in the summer of 1990, and that fall Viking brought out the first American edition. Like *The Giraffe and the Pelly and Me, Esio Trot* is fairly short, is illustrated by Quentin Blake, and has a gentler tone than most of Dahl's other children's books.

Child characters do not play significant roles in *Esio Trot*. Instead, the story focuses on two adults: Mr. Hoppy, a retired mechanic who loves gardening, and Mrs. Silver, a middle-aged widow who has a pet tortoise named Alfie. Both Mr. Hoppy and Mrs. Silver live in a high-rise apartment building, and Mr. Hoppy's apartment is directly above Mrs. Silver's. Mr. Hoppy is secretly in love with Mrs. Silver, but he is too shy to ask her out or even to talk to her for more than a few minutes.

The plot revolves around Mr. Hoppy's unusual approach to winning the affections of his downstairs neighbor. During one of their brief conversations she tells him that she is distressed because Alfie has gained only three ounces in 11 years. She then tells Mr. Hoppy that if he could figure out a way to make Alfie grow a little faster, she would be his "slave for life." Encouraged by this offhand remark, Mr. Hoppy says that he knows a secret technique to make tortoises grow, and he agrees to share it with her. Tortoises, according to Mr. Hoppy, are backward creatures, and they only understand words when they are said backwards. He then writes down some strange-looking words and instructs Mrs. Silver to chant them to Alfie three times a day. The chant begins, "ESIO TROT, ESIO TROT, TEG REGGIB REGGIB!"[23] As Mr. Hoppy explains to the bewildered Mrs. Silver, Alfie will understand these words to mean "TORTOISE, TORTOISE, GET BIGGER BIGGER!" Mrs. Silver is intrigued with Mr. Hoppy's technique and agrees to follow his instructions.

Mr. Hoppy knows that everything he has told Mrs. Silver about tortoises is simply gibberish, but he embarks on an elaborate campaign to convince her that his technique really works. He buys 140 tortoises of various sizes and keeps them all in his apartment. One day, while Mrs. Silver is at work, he replaces Alfie with a tortoise that is slightly bigger. He repeats this operation every week for eight weeks. Since tortoises look so much alike, Mrs. Silver never realizes that she is being fooled. At the end of this process Mr. Hoppy suggests that Mrs. Silver reweigh her tortoise, and she is thrilled to discover that it has doubled in size. She calls Mr. Hoppy the "most wonderful man" she has ever met (*Esio,* 57) and invites him to tea, and soon thereafter the two are married.

*Esio Trot* differs from Dahl's other books for young readers in several important ways. It is the only one that does not contain any fantasy elements. Parts of it are rather farfetched, but everything that happens in the story could conceivably happen in the real world. *Esio Trot* is also the most adult-oriented of these books. Not only are the major characters adults; they also deal with adult concerns. The absence of a villain also separates *Esio Trot* from the rest of Dahl's children's books.

Although children generally like the fantasy elements, child characters, and villains found in most of Dahl's children's books, they also appreciate certain qualities of *Esio Trot.* The book has a fast-paced and carefully constructed plot, many humorous scenes, some amusing wordplay, and lots of comical illustrations. Nevertheless, compared to the rest of Dahl's books for younger children, this one does not appeal as strongly to its intended audience. Several reviewers picked up on this point. The reviewer for *Publishers Weekly,* for example, enjoyed the book but felt that its "subtle humor" would appeal primarily to "adults and older children."[24] It would be a mistake, however, to describe *Esio Trot* as an adult book masquerading as a children's book. This description does apply to *The Vicar of Nibbleswicke,* a story that Dahl wrote shortly after finishing *Esio Trot,* but Dahl clearly intended *Esio Trot* for young readers.

## The Minpins

In a letter written a few months before his death, Dahl referred to his last children's book, *The Minpins,* as a fairy tale. Since he did not refer to his other works for children as fairy tales, his use of the term to describe *The Minpins* suggests that he saw it as being significantly different from the rest. This notion is further supported by a note he wrote on the title page of the manuscript: "This story requires beautiful and detailed illustrations." Thus, while Dahl generally liked the way Quentin Blake illustrated his books, he clearly did not think that Blake's cartoonish style would capture the spirit of this book. Jonathan Cape honored his request and arranged to have the book illustrated by Patrick Benson. Cape published the book in 1991, and Viking published the first American edition the same year.

*The Minpins* is one of Dahl's only works for children in which humor does not play a major role. It is a serious story about the lure of danger, the bravery of a young boy, and the magical secrets of a forbidding forest. It includes a few funny scenes, but they are restrained and do not dispel the story's mystical quality. Though so different in tone from most of Dahl's writings, *The Minpins* has some interesting connections with a number of his earlier works, including *The Giraffe and the Pelly and Me, The Gremlins,* and *The Magic Finger.*

The protagonist is Little Billy, the same character who appears in *The Giraffe and the Pelly and Me.* Little Billy and his mother live in a house at the edge of The Forest of Sin. Little Billy longs to explore the forest, but his mother forbids it. She says that the forest is filled with horrible beasts, the worst of which is the Terrible Bloodsuckling Toothpluckling Stonechuckling Spittler, but her warnings only make the forest sound more enticing to Little Billy.

One day he disobeys his mother and ventures into the forest. At first the forest seems deadly quiet, but after a while he starts to hear some ominous sounds. As the sounds grow louder he realizes that they are coming from a creature. He cannot really see what the creature looks like, because it is surrounded by clouds of steam and smoke, but he instinctively knows that the creature is pursuing him. He runs away, but the creature keeps getting closer. Finally, Little Billy leaps into a tree and climbs out of the creature's reach. While resting in the tree he makes a startling discovery: tiny windows are cut into the bark of the tree, and light is coming out of them. He soon learns that this hollow tree is home to a group of tiny people called the Minpins.

The Minpins are strikingly similar to the little people that Dahl wrote about in his 1943 book *The Gremlins*. Both the Minpins and the gremlins are only a few inches high. Both groups live in remote forests and avoid contact with humans. Perhaps the oddest characteristic they share is their footgear: they both wear suction boots that enable them to walk up the sides of tree trunks and to stroll upside down along tree branches. In terms of appearance the only major difference between the two groups is that the gremlins have horns and the Minpins do not.

Little Billy meets Don Mini, the leader of the Minpins, who tells him that the Minpins inhabit the entire forest but that they, like Little Billy, cannot leave the trees without risking being eaten by the same creature that chased Little Billy. The Minpins avoid this creature, which they call the Red-Hot Smoke-Belching Gruncher, by relying on birds to take them where they need to go. As Don Mini explains, the Minpins store food for the birds, and in return the birds allow the Minpins to ride on their backs.

Using the information that Don Mini has given him about the Gruncher's ways, Little Billy devises a plan to rid the forest of the dreaded monster. His plan requires that Don Mini find a bird that is large enough to carry Little Billy, and Don Mini has no problem meeting this requirement. He summons a swan that agrees to help Little Billy implement his daring plan. After his plan succeeds, Little Billy becomes a hero to the Minpins and returns home without his mother knowing that he had ever entered the forest. The Minpins reward him by arranging to have the swan fly to his window every night and take him on wondrous rides. Although Little Billy and the swan cannot speak to each other, they form a loving relationship. Little Billy is not the only child from a Dahl story to have special connections with the animal world. The girl in *The Magic Finger* feels such strong ties to animals that she becomes their protector. Similarly, the central character in the short story "The Boy Who Could Talk with Animals," one of the stories anthologized in *The Wonderful Story of Henry Sugar and Six More,* forms a magical bond with a giant sea turtle that he rescues. Little Billy is actually the second Dahl character to feel close to a swan. The first is Peter Watson in "The Swan," another story included in *The Wonderful Story of Henry Sugar.* Although "The Swan" is directed at an older audience than *The Minpins,* both stories feature boys who relate to swans on an almost spiritual level.

Another way in which *The Minpins* relates to Dahl's other children's books is in its use of fantasy. Like most of his children's books, *The Minpins* is set in what seems to be the real world, but this realistic setting does not preclude magic—at least not for those who are willing to look for it. The mother in *The Minpins* is not willing to look. For her and for many of the adults in Dahl's children's books, the world is a mundane place. But for Little Billy and most of Dahl's other child characters, the world is a wondrous land in which amazing things can happen. This theme runs through nearly all of Dahl's fiction for children, but it is perhaps stated most explicitly in the conclusion to *The Minpins.* In a sense this passage, which is addressed directly to the reader, serves as Dahl's parting words to his young audience: "Watch with glittering eyes the whole world around you because the greatest secrets are always hidden in the most unlikely places. Those who don't believe in magic will never find it."[25]

# 7

# Versifying

Dahl's first children's book, *The Gremlins,* concludes with a big celebration, during which a group of jubilant gremlins sing the following lines:

> Wipple Scrumpet in the sky,
> Wipple Scrumpet in the sky,
> Pilots all were born to fly
> Higher than the highest high—
> Wipple Scrumpet in the sky.
> (*Gremlins*)

These are but the first of many lines of verse that Dahl wrote for children. In four of his children's books—*James and the Giant Peach, Charlie and the Chocolate Factory, Charlie and the Great Glass Elevator,* and *The Giraffe and the Pelly and Me*—lines of verse are spliced into the text at fairly regular intervals. Like the poems in Lewis Carroll's *Alice's Adventures in Wonderland,* the verses in these four books are humorous and are intended to supplement the prose. Dahl also wrote several books of verse. The first of these, *Roald Dahl's Revolting Rhymes,* came out in 1982.

This was followed by *Dirty Beasts,* published in 1983, and *Rhyme Stew,* published in 1989.

## Supplemental Verse

Although Dahl included a few lines of verse in *The Gremlins,* it was not until he wrote *James and the Giant Peach* that he fully developed this aspect of his writing. In *James and the Giant Peach* there are six poems. Two of them are only a few stanzas long, but the others go on for several pages. Some are couplets, some are limericks, and some follow more complex rhyme schemes. The poems also vary in terms of meter. Iambic meter tends to predominate, but some of the poems follow other rhythmic patterns. Indeed, even the poems that seem to be written in iambic meter usually contain a few lines that deviate from this pattern. No matter what form the poems take, however, they all have a strong beat that works well when they are read aloud.

Since all of the poems in *James and the Giant Peach* are written in the voices of particular characters, they help define the characters' personalities. In the first poem Aunt Sponge and Aunt Spiker each describes herself as a ravishing beauty while describing the other in much less flattering terms. Although the poem presents both characters in a comical light, it underscores their extreme self-centeredness. Most of the other poems are sung by the Centipede. Of all the insects in the story, the Centipede is the most aggressive, and this attribute is accentuated in his songs. In one song he takes great pleasure in recounting the demise of the aunts, and in another he proudly calls himself "the most marvelous pest" (*James,* 99). One of the Centipede's other attributes is his total disregard for social niceties. He takes pleasure in things that most people would find repulsive. This aspect of his personality comes to the fore when he sings about his favorite foods:

> I crave the tasty tentacles of octopi for tea
> I like hot-dogs, I LOVE hot-frogs, and surely

you'll agree
A plate of soil with engine oil's
A super recipe.
(*James,* 53)

Like Edward Lear's famous limericks, the poems in *James and the Giant Peach* often make comic references to death and violence. At one point, for example, the Centipede sings:

We may even get lost and be frozen by frost.
We may die in an earthquake or tremor.
Or nastier still, we may even be tossed
On the horns of a furious Dilemma.
(*James,* 38)

In comparison to the prose passages, the poems are generally more violent and a bit wilder. These poems, however, are not especially frightening or threatening, because the violence is undercut with humor. Moreover, the wildness of the poems is counterbalanced by their structured form and stylized language.

The verse in *Charlie and the Chocolate Factory* is not nearly as varied in form or function as that in *James and the Giant Peach.* All the poems in *Charlie and the Chocolate Factory* are couplets, and they are all written in iambic tetrameter. One is recited by Willy Wonka, and the rest are sung by the Oompa-Loompas. Although there is much humor in the Oompa-Loompa's songs, their primary function is to draw out the moral implications behind some of the key events in the story. The Oompa-Loompas break into song every time something disastrous happens to one of the obnoxious children. Their songs generally start off with descriptions of the children's behavioral flaws. When, for example, the gluttonous Agustus Gloop is sucked up into a giant pipe, the Oompa-Loompas sing a song that begins with the following lines:

Agustus Gloop! Agustus Gloop!
The great big greedy nincompoop!
How long could we allow this beast
To gorge and guzzle, feed and feast

On everything he wanted to?
Great Scott! It simply wouldn't do!
However long this pig might live
We're positive he'd never give
Even the smallest bit of fun
Or happiness to anyone.
(*Chocolate*, 84)

There is considerable variation among the verses in *Charlie and the Great Glass Elevator*. Two of the poems follow an *abab* rhyme scheme, and the others use different verse forms. They all, however, are written in a style that works best when read aloud. Unlike the poems in the first *Charlie* book, the poems in this book are not associated with a particular character or set of characters. These poems are recited by Willy Wonka, the Oompa-Loompas, and Miss Tibbs, the president's nanny, among other characters.

Although they vary in terms of form and voice, most of these poems include scatological humor. One deals with a monster who seems to be suffering from hemorrhoids, and another refers to the president's toilet training. The longest poem in the book is about a girl who takes an overdose of her grandmother's laxatives. As a result of this rash act, the girl has to spend countless hours "Within the everlasting gloom / Of what we call The Ladies Room" (*Glass*, 49).

The scatological humor found in most of the verse does not figure in the book's first poem. Willy Wonka, the character who gives voice to this poem, is trying to sound like a dangerous creature from another planet. The poem therefore includes many nonsensical but ominous-sounding words:

In the quelchy quaggy sogmire,
In the mashy mideous harshland,
At the witchy hour of gloomness,
All the grobes come oozing home.
(*Glass*, 49)

Although it goes on for only two more stanzas, this poem is arguably one of Dahl's most noteworthy. Compared with his other poems, it has a more serious tone and makes more extensive use of nonsense words. In both tone and language this poem moves in the direction of Lewis Carroll's "Jabberwocky." In its use of nonsense words it also has similarities to some of Edward Lear's longer poems, such as "The Owl and the Pussy Cat."

*The Giraffe and the Pelly and Me* is far shorter than *James and the Giant Peach* or either of the two *Charlie* books, but there are more poems in it than in any of these others. Although all three of the animal characters in the story recite at least one poem, the Monkey is the one who is most inclined to poetry. All of the poems that are attributed to the Monkey, as well as several of the other poems in the book, follow an *aabccb* rhyme scheme. The six-line stanzas usually end with the same line that serves as the title of the book. In fact, the first thing that the Monkey says adheres to this pattern:

> We will polish your glass
> Till it's shining like brass
> And it sparkles like sun on the sea!
> We are quick and polite,
> We will come day or night,
> The Giraffe and the Pelly and me![1]
> (*Giraffe*)

The poems in this book serve a somewhat different function than those in most of Dahl's other children's books. Rather than comment on events in the story, these poems help tell the story. Several important plot elements are explained in the poems, including the details of the animals' window-cleaning business. Because these poems are tied so closely to the narrative, they cannot be fully appreciated if read apart from the story.

## Books of Verse

Dahl's three books of verse—*Roald Dahl's Revolting Rhymes, Dirty Beasts,* and *Rhyme Stew*—are much alike. The same verse form is used in all three books. With the exception of a few of the poems in *Rhyme Stew*, these books consist of lengthy couplets written in iambic tetrameter. The verses in these books are also similar in tone; they all are satirical and rather ribald. In most cases they play havoc with the conventions of traditional children's literature.

In 1982 Jonathan Cape published *Roald Dahl's Revolting Rhymes* with Quentin Blake's colorful illustrations, and the next year Knopf brought out the book in America. The book consists of parodies of six classic fairy tales: "Cinderella," "Snow White and the Seven Dwarfs," "Jack and the Beanstalk," "Goldilocks and the Three Bears," "Little Red Riding Hood," and "The Three Little Pigs." Like Lewis Carroll's famous parodies of Victorian poems, Dahl's parodies of fairy tales feature all sorts of absurd situations and much comic violence.

Dahl's versions of the fairy tales differ from the originals in several amusing ways. Although both versions usually begin with the same premise, Dahl's versions always have surprise endings. Cinderella, for example, rejects the prince in favor of a poor man who makes "good homemade marmalade."[2] Dahl's anachronistic references to aspects of the modern world also distinguish his versions from the traditional tales. In Dahl's rendition of "Snow White and the Seven Dwarfs," for example, the dwarfs have "squandered all their resources / At the race track backing horses" (*Revolting*, 15). In some of Dahl's parodies the surprise endings hinge on the introduction of modern devices. This is certainly the case in his conclusion to "Little Red Riding Hood." In Dahl's version, as in James Thurber's version from his *Fables for Our Time*, the wolf discovers that Little Red Riding Hood has an unexpected resource at her disposal:

> The small girl smiles. One eye flickers.
> She whips a pistol from her knickers.
> She aims it at the creature's head.
> And *bang bang bang,* she shoots him dead.
> A few weeks later, in the wood,
> I came across Miss Riding Hood.
> But what a change! No cloak of red,
> No silly hood upon her head.

She said, "Hello, and do please note
My lovely furry wolfskin coat."
(*Revolting*, 32)

The critical reaction to *Roald Dahl's Revolting Rhymes* was quite mixed. Trev Jones lambasted the book in a review published in the *School Library Journal*. Jones wrote, "Dahl's tampering of these familiar folk tales is just what the title implies—revolting. Bathroom humor, violence and name calling predominate. While many sixth to eighth graders respond to these elements of humor, the selection question is: must adults pander to this level of taste?"[3] Thomas M. Disch, who reviewed the book for the *Washington Post Book World*, did not find the poems offensive, but he disliked Dahl's writing style. According to Disch, Dahl's "doggerel couplets have a numbing one-and-two-and-now-we're-through monotony that has the bumpy effect, over long stretches, of riding an octogonal-wheeled bicycle."[4] Some reviewers, however, liked the book. Andrew Hislop, for example, gave it high praise in a review published in the *Times Literary Supplement*. In Hislop's opinion, "*Revolting Rhymes* is in fact pure pleasure. Raucous, irreverent, inventive, richly colloquial in its language, never afraid to press-gang the inappropriate into its service, it delights with its teasing turns of phrase and twists of plot."[5]

Dahl's second book of verse, *Dirty Beasts*, has a rather unusual publishing history. Unlike some of Dahl's other children's books from the 1980s, *Dirty Beasts* appeared in America and England in the same year. In 1983 Jonathan Cape released the book in Great Britain while Farrar, Straus & Giroux brought out the American edition. Both of these editions feature illustrations by Rosemary Fawcett. In 1984, though, Cape published another edition of the book, for which Quentin Blake supplied the illustrations.

*Dirty Beasts*, as its title implies, consists of poems about animals. In all of the book's nine poems, the featured animals have some sort of conflict with humans. Like the animals in *Fantastic Mr. Fox*, the beasts in these poems are not passive victims of human cruelty and aggression. Indeed, they prove to be more than a match for the humans in the poems. The book begins with a poem about a pig who comes to the realization that the farmer who feeds him intends to eat him eventually. The pig therefore decides to eat the farmer first. Eating people seems like a good idea to several of the book's other beasts, including a crocodile, a lion, and an anteater. Although the remaining beasts do not see people as potential meals, they certainly do not treat humans with much respect. In one poem, for example, a flying cow revenges herself upon a man who makes fun of her for flying:

> She dived, and using all her power
> She got to sixty mile an hour.
> "Bombs gone!" she cried. "Take that!" she said,
> And dropped a cowpat on his head.[6]

The humor in *Dirty Beasts* draws on several sources. In some of the poems the humor comes from presenting threatening beasts in a silly light. This is clearly the case with the poem about the crocodile. Even though the crocodile likes to eat children, he goes about it in such an amusing way that the whole business seems funny rather than scary. In some of the other poems, such as the one about the flying cow, the humor is of a scatological nature. The type of humor associated with wordplay also figures in some of the poems. The poem about the anteater, for example, is based on an extended pun. One day the boy who owns the anteater introduces his 83-year-old aunt to his pet, and the result is instant mayhem:

> The creature smiled. Its tummy rumbled.
> It licked its starving lips and mumbled,
> "A giant ant! By gosh, a winner!
> "At last I'll get a decent dinner!
> "No matter if it's eighty-three.
> "If that's an ant, then it's for me!"
> Then, taking very careful aim,
> It pounced upon the startled dame.
> It grabbed her firmly by the hair
> And ate her up right then and there.
> (*Dirty*)

Most of the critics who reviewed *Dirty Beasts* did not appreciate the book's humor. The reviewer for the *Economist* liked the idea of having animals take revenge on people but felt that Dahl did not make that idea work. As the reviewer put it, "There could be a certain humour in this reversal of roles but Roald Dahl has preferred to leave it out."[7] Maria Salvadore, a reviewer for the *School Library Journal,* was even harsher in her assessment of the book. "The attempt at humor," she wrote, "fails. The result is sadistic, predictable, and very unfunny."[8] Although the reviewers who disliked the book greatly outnumbered those who liked it, a few did find the book funny. In the *Times Literary Supplement* Candida Lycett Green argued that although the book's humor might not appeal to adults, "it is music to children's ears."[9]

Dahl's third book of verse, *Rhyme Stew,* was released by his British publisher, Jonathan Cape, in the fall of 1989. In April 1990 Viking published the first American edition of the book. Quentin Blake's black-and-white illustrations accompany both editions. Both also feature a label that reads, "Warning: Unsuitable for Small Readers." The publishers took the unusual step of putting this warning on the cover because some of the book's poems have vague sexual connotations.

A bit longer than Dahl's two previous collections of verse, *Rhyme Stew* contains 15 poems. The six longest are parodies of well-known fairy or folk tales, including "The Tortoise and the Hare," "The Emperor's New Clothes," "Hansel and Gretel," and "Aladdin and the Magic Lamp." The book also includes brief parodies of three famous nursery rhymes: "St. Ives," "Hey Diddle Diddle," and "Mary, Mary." The remaining six poems are more like the poems in *Dirty Beasts* in that they are freestanding works rather than parodies of traditional children's stories or poems.

The six parodies of fairy tales are very similar to the poems in *Roald Dahl's Revolting Rhymes.* Not only are all these poems written in the form of couplets, but they are also irreverent and ribald. The fairy-tale parodies in *Rhyme Stew,* like the earlier parodies, generally include comic violence, references to modern machines and institutions, and surprise endings. All of these elements are clearly evident in Dahl's version of "The Tortoise and the Hare."

In this scenario Tortoise secretly hires Rat, the local mechanic, to build "A little four-wheeled car / That travels fast and very far."[10] Tortoise then pays Rat to attach the tiny car beneath his shell "in such a way no man can tell" (*Stew,* 23). Rat builds the car, but he sells his secret information to Hare, who in turn hires Rat to disable Tortoise's car during the race. Rat accomplishes this by scattering nails over the road. The nails stop Tortoise by puncturing his tires, but they also puncture Hare's feet, thus preventing him from finishing the race as well. In the end, the only one who profits from the race is Rat, a point emphasized in the poem's concluding lines:

> So just remember if you can,
> Don't tangle with a business man.
> It doesn't matter who you choose,
> They always win, we always lose.
> If you were here and I was there,
> If you were Tortoise, I was Hare,
> We'd both get diddled in the end
> By people like our Ratty friend.
> (*Stew,* 29)

The nursery-rhyme parodies use the opening lines from the original verses, but then they spin off in unexpected directions. In Dahl's version of "St. Ives" the mathematical riddling found in the original is not present. Instead, the "man with seven wives" extols the joys of polygamy (*Stew,* 16). The parody of "Hey Diddle Diddle" has absolutely nothing to do with a musical cat or a jumping cow; the characters are some shady workers who "only take cash." The humor in this poem hinges on the phrase "on the fiddle" (*Stew,* 55), which is British slang for cheating or ignoring societal rules. Dahl's "Mary, Mary," begins with the familiar question about her garden, but her answer breaks with tradition: "I live with my brat in a high-rise flat, / So how in the world would I know" (*Stew,* 55).

The other poems in *Rhyme Stew* vary considerably in length, verse form, and subject matter. Most of them, however, have at least one point in common; they touch on the subject of sexuality.

In a poem called "A Hand in a Bird," a woman working at a church bazaar feels something crawling up her thigh. She makes a grab for it, thinking it is a mouse, only to discover that it is the vicar's hand. A poem entitled "The Price of Debauchery" begins with a mother warning her daughter that if she kisses boys, she will catch some "foul disease." The girl kisses a boy anyway, and sure enough, she catches his "runny cold" (*Stew,* 30). Another poem features a female gym teacher who asks one of her male students to stay after class so that she can teach him some unusual wrestling holds. In the book's final poem, "Hot and Cold," a woman starts undressing in front of a boy. The boy is concerned that she might be getting cold, but the woman says, "Indeed I'm not! / I'm feeling devilishly hot!" (*Stew,* 45)

With the exception of "A Hand in the Bird," Dahl's poems that refer to sexuality are told from a child's point of view. In many ways the voices used in these poems sound like those of real children. Although some adults try to deny it, sexuality often figures in children's jokes and rhymes. As Francelia Butler pointed out in *Skipping Around the World,* sexual humor can be found in many of the rhymes that children say when they think that adults are not listening. "Some adults are surprised," Butler wrote, "to learn that many children's rhymes, including those for skipping, have an unmistakably sexual, sometimes even bawdy, element. In some, the bawdy aspect is too broad to appeal to refined tastes."[11] The sexual humor in Dahl's poems is much like the humor in jump-rope rhymes. In both cases the humor is intended to demystify sex and make fun of sexually active adults.

*Rhyme Stew* received lukewarm endorsements from a few reviewers, but most of the adults who wrote about the book disapproved of it with varying degrees of intensity. One of the positive responses came from Patricia Dooley, who reviewed the book for *Library Journal.* Dooley wrote, "The usual Dahl ingredients, irreverent wit and comic invention liberally spiced with the mildly suggestive or *outré,* suit this stew to the popular (if unrefined) taste of adolescents of every age."[12] The reviewer for *Publishers Weekly* gave the book a more negative review but did not denounce it. This reviewer simply called Dahl's verses "sophomoric" and wrote that his "attempts at playful lasciviousness seem juvenile."[13] In a similar vein, D. J. Enright, a reviewer for the *Times Literary Supplement,* found the book repetitive and "dispiriting."[14] One of the most negative reactions came from Mary Smith. In a lengthy piece published in the London *Times* Smith argued that Dahl's book encourages child sexual abuse. She focused her argument on the poem about the female gym teacher who wrestles with her male student. In Smith's opinion the teacher's behavior "is a form of abuse" that is "not funny for the victims." Smith concluded by accusing Dahl of "contradict[ing] the painstaking work of many caring professionals."[15]

Of all Dahl's books, his collections of verse drew the harshest response from established reviewers and critics. For the most part these reviewers based their negative reactions on what they perceived to be the books' tastelessness. The issue of taste, however, is a matter that generally concerns adults much more than it does children. As Dahl well knew, what offends adults often delights children. His books of verse are designed to provide children with such forbidden delights. Thus, there is a generational element involved in the controversy surrounding Dahl's books of verse. The reviewers in some ways represent the propriety of adulthood, while Dahl represents the crudity of childhood.

# 8

# Writing from Life

Dahl began his writing career with an autobiographical essay about the time his fighter plane crashed in Libya. After the publication of that essay in 1942, however, Dahl did not return to autobiographical writing for over 20 years. His next effort in that area, an article entitled "My Wife, Patricia Neal," appeared in the September 1965 issue of *Ladies' Home Journal*. Although he focused this article on the events surrounding Neal's stroke, he also briefly described the routines and crises that had shaped their family life before her stroke. It was not until the mid-1970s, however, that Dahl wrote a detailed account of his formative years. He called this piece "Lucky Break: How I Became a Writer," and he included it in his anthology *The Wonderful Story of Henry Sugar and Six More*. This essay proved to be a precursor to two autobiographical books. The first of these, *Boy: Tales of Childhood*, was published in 1984 by both Jonathan Cape, who released the British edition, and Farrar, Straus & Giroux, who brought out the American edition. In 1986 the same publishers released Dahl's second autobiographical book, *Going Solo*.

In the hands of practically any writer, the story of Dahl's eventful life would make for interesting reading, but Dahl's accounts of his early years are more than just interesting. Almost all the critics who reviewed *Boy* and *Going Solo* found the books captivating. The reviewers of *Boy* used phrases such as "superbly written"[1] and "very readable and quite fascinating,"[2] while the reviewers of *Going Solo* praised Dahl's "expert raconteurship"[3] and ability to tell a story "that rivets the attention."[4] As several reviewers mentioned, Dahl's autobiographical writings have many of the same qualities that make his fiction so readable. They are fast-paced narratives in which the action is smoothly combined with unusual details and astute and sometimes disturbing observations.

The connections between Dahl's autobiographical works and his fictional works transcend similarities in writing style. Many of the places, people, and events described in his autobiographies have parallels in his short stories and children's books. In some cases the parallels are direct and obvious. Many of the events described in *Going Solo*, for example, are clearly the basis for some of the short stories in *Over to You*. In other cases, though, the parallels are not so readily apparent. Still, for those who are familiar with Dahl's short stories and especially with his children's books, reading his autobiographies is much like experiencing déjà vu.

Certain places in which Dahl lived figure strongly in both his autobiographical writings and his fiction. One of these places is Norway. Some of the most memorable pages in *Boy* deal with the summers that Dahl spent with his family on a little island off the coast of Norway. As detailed in *Boy*, even as a young child Dahl appreciated the beauty of Norway's rugged fjords and rocky islands. He also loved visiting his Norwegian grandparents, who lived in what is now Oslo. His grandparents exposed him to some of the foods, customs, and legends of Norway, all of which he found fascinating.

Dahl's childhood visits to Norway provided him with much of the background material that he later used in *The Witches*. In addition to drawing on Norwegian legends and folklore about witches, Dahl worked some of his own Norwegian experiences into the story. Indeed, the young boy in the story learns about Norway in much the same way that Dahl learned about it as a child. The following passage from *The Witches*, for example, comes close to describing Dahl's experience: "My grandmother was Norwegian. . . . My father and my mother were also Norwegian, but because my father had a business in England, I had been born there and had lived there and had started going to an English school. Twice a year, at Christmas and in the summer, we went back to Norway to visit my grandmother" (*Witches,* 9–10).

The concluding pages of *Boy* and the first few chapters of *Going Solo* describe how Dahl became enthralled with another faraway place—East Africa. *Boy* ends with Dahl learning that his new employer, the Shell Oil Company, plans to send him to their branch office in East Africa. As Dahl recalled in *Boy,* when he heard this news he felt so happy that he just started shouting, "Lions! And elephants and giraffes and coconuts everywhere!" (*Boy,* 158). In *Going Solo* Dahl explains how his initial infatuation with Africa developed into a genuine appreciation for the area once he actually started living there.

Dahl's interest in Africa has shown up in his fiction on several occasions. Toward the beginning of his writing career, for example, he wrote a short story entitled "An African Story," which focuses on a large and poisonous African snake called the mamba. Although the story's plot is fictional, Dahl actually had a harrowing experience with a mamba, which is described in *Going Solo.* Africa also serves as the setting for *The Enormous Crocodile* and figures in the first version of *Charlie and the Chocolate Factory.* African animals play major roles in several of Dahl's other children's books, including *The Twits* and *The Giraffe and the Pelly and Me.* In Dahl's fiction Africa retains the exciting and almost magical qualities that he first associated with the area during his youth.

Connections between Dahl's autobiographical writings and his fiction go well beyond the bounds of geography. A number of the people mentioned in *Boy* can be recognized in several of Dahl's fictional works. The most notable examples are some of the harsh adults with whom Dahl came into contact after his mother sent him to boarding school. One was the woman who supervised the boys in Dahl's dormitory during his first year away from home. An entire chapter of *Boy* is devoted to describing this cruel woman and her sadistic but creative forms of punishment. Once, for example, she put flakes of soap into a snoring boy's open mouth in order to teach him not to sleep on his back. In terms of both her appearance and her behavior toward children, this woman is strikingly similar to Miss Trunchbull, the cruel headmistress in *Matilda.*

Another chapter in *Boy* focuses on some of the older boys that Dahl met when he started attending Repton. These boys, the Boazers, forced Dahl and the other younger students to do humiliating tasks. If the tasks were not performed to the Boazers' satisfaction, they beat the younger boys. The Boazers are described in detail in *Boy,* and they also appear in Dahl's short story "Galloping Foxley." In that story one particularly cruel Boazer torments another student to such an extent that the Boazer's victim is still troubled by the experience some 50 years later. The tactics that the Boazer uses in the story are the same ones used by the Boazers at Repton.

Sometimes the connections between Dahl's autobiographical writings and his fictional works have more to do with events than with places or people. For instance, the chapter in *Boy* entitled "Chocolates" focuses on one of Dahl's few pleasant experiences during his stay at Repton. On occasion Dahl and the other students were asked to taste-test chocolate bars made by the famous Cadbury Chocolate Company. Apparently, the company's product-development division often tried out their new chocolate bars on students before putting them on the market. While munching on these candy bars the young Dahl would fantasize about working in the inventing room of a large chocolate company. These fantasies, as Dahl readily admitted in *Boy,* eventually found their way into one of his most popular children's books: "It was lovely dreaming those dreams, and I have no doubt at all that, thirty-five years later, when I was looking for a plot for my second book for children, I remembered those little cardboard boxes and the newly-invented chocolates inside them, and I began to write a book called *Charlie and the Chocolate Factory*" (*Boy,* 135).

Some of Dahl's other books also appear to have grown from his fantasies about concocting new kinds of chocolates. In *My Uncle*

*Oswald* the title character adds a powerful aphrodisiac to some chocolate truffles and then tricks some unsuspecting men into eating the doctored candies. Similarily, the Grand High Witch in *The Witches* plans to use doctored chocolates in her campaign to turn all of the children in England into mice. She wants to put drops of her "Formula 86 Delayed-Action Mouse-Maker" concoction into thousands of chocolates and then give the chocolates to children (*Witches,* 78). Although the chocolates in these two books are more dangerous than most of the candies in *Charlie and the Chocolate Factory,* all three books recall Dahl's childhood perception of chocolate as something that transcends everyday reality.

Testing chocolates for Cadbury is but one of many events that link Dahl's autobiographical writings to his fiction, but these incidents pale in significance when compared with the overarching value system that ties together all of Dahl's writings. Key parts of this system are Dahl's cynical view of social institutions, his belief that individuals should not automatically adhere to societal norms and expectations, and his tendency to see the family as a possible source of happiness and comfort.

The origins of Dahl's cynicism toward social institutions and societal norms can be seen in both *Boy* and *Going Solo.* Much of *Boy* deals with Dahl's unhappy experiences at the schools that he attended. As a child he recoiled at the schools' regimentation and frequent use of corporal punishment. He also intensely disliked his authoritarian teachers. Even as a child Dahl felt that these teachers cared more about maintaining quiet and orderly classrooms that they did about educating their students. During the period of his life covered in *Going Solo* Dahl began to question the wisdom of the military leaders who commanded him while he was a pilot in the RAF. He knew that he had to obey these men, but he sometimes felt that their orders made little sense. His educational and military experiences predisposed Dahl to take a negative view of all social forces that try to coerce people into following a uniform system of thought and behavior.

In almost all of Dahl's fiction authoritarian figures, social institutions, and societal norms are ridiculed or at least undermined. Many of his children's books satirize authoritarian adults, and some, such as *Matilda,* include stinging attacks on schools and other institutions. Most of his children's books also poke fun at the propriety of the adult world. In these books adult notions of what is proper and in good taste come across as being hypocritical and dehumanizing. Like his children's books, Dahl's stories for adults criticize social norms, but they do so in a somewhat different way. These stories generally show how meaningless life can be when conforming to societal norms is the primary motivating force in people's lives. For the most part the characters in these stories appear to be respectable members of society, but they are basically unethical and uncaring people. So long as they are able to rely on societal norms to govern their behavior they seem civilized enough, but as soon as these norms break down they quickly become savages.

There is one major exception to Dahl's pessimistic view of social structures, and that is his attitude toward the family. As is made clear in *Boy* and *Going Solo,* the happiest moments of Dahl's youth were those spent with his family. During his years at boarding school he saw his family as a sort of oasis in an otherwise hostile world. Even when he was working in Africa or flying in the RAF, he tried to stay in close contact with his family. Every week, for example, he wrote a letter to his mother.

Dahl's sense of the importance of families is reflected in his fiction. In most of his adult stories families are conspicuously absent. There are many couples in his stories, but most of them do not have children. This absence of families is in keeping with the meaninglessness of these characters' lives. Perhaps if they had children they would not be so self-centered and obsessed with their social status. Families, however, do figure in several of Dahl's children's books. In the case of *Matilda* the family is not much more than a collection of individuals who live in the same house, but the families in some of his other children's books are much more like the family that Dahl knew as a child. The family of foxes in *Fantastic Mr. Fox,* the father and son in *Danny, the Champion of the World,* and the grandmother and grandson in *The Witches* all have loving and close relationships. The members of these families are often at odds with the rest of the world, but they always support each other. Thus, even though Dahl's fiction presents a pessimistic view of modern civilization, it holds out hope that individuals can find happiness and meaning within the bosoms of their own families.

Dahl's fiction clearly reflects his values and beliefs, but he seldom discussed this aspect of his writing. When interviewers questioned him about his vision of human nature or the meaning of his stories, he generally gave evasive answers. If pressed he argued that the job of analyzing his stories rested with critics and scholars; his job, he maintained, was simply to entertain his readers. During one of his last interviews, however, he admitted that entertainment was not his only goal as a children's author:

> When I'm writing for adults, I'm just trying to entertain them. But a good children's book does much more than entertain. It teaches children the use of words, the joy of playing with language. Above all, it helps children learn not to be frightened of books. Once they can get through a book and enjoy it, they realize that books are something that they can cope with. If they are going to amount to anything in life, they need to be able to handle books. If my books can help children become readers, then I feel I have accomplished something important. (West 1990, 65–66)

As one of the most popular children's authors in the Western world and certainly the best-selling one from England, Dahl helped turn countless children into avid readers. This accomplishment gave him greater satisfaction than the critical acclaim he earned or the awards he won. The immense popularity of his children's books also guarantees that Dahl's work, despite its controversial nature, will leave a lasting mark on the history of children's literature.

# Notes and References

## Chapter One

1. Lewis Nichols, "Child's Dahl," *New York Times Book Review,* 23 April 1961, 8; hereafter cited in text.
2. Mark I. West, "Interview with Roald Dahl," *Children's Literature in Education* 21 (June 1990): 65; hereafter cited in text.
3. Roald Dahl, *Boy: Tales of Childhood* (New York: Farrar, Straus & Giroux, 1984), 50; hereafter cited in text as *Boy.*
4. Roald Dahl, "Lucky Break—How I Became a Writer," in *The Wonderful Story of Henry Sugar and Six More* (New York: Knopf, 1977), 184; hereafter cited in text as *Wonderful.*
5. Roald Dahl, *Going Solo* (New York: Farrar, Straus & Giroux, 1986), 32.
6. John Terraine, *A Time for Courage: The Royal Air Force in the European War, 1939–1945* (New York: Macmillan, 1985), 325–34.
7. Chris Powling, *Roald Dahl* (Middlesex, England: Puffin, 1985), 43; hereafter cited in text.
8. Justin Wintle and Emma Fisher, *The Pied Piper: Interviews with the Influential Creators of Children's Literature* (New York: Paddington Press, 1974), 103–4; hereafter cited in text.
9. Barry Farrell, *Pat and Roald* (New York: Random House, 1969), 70; hereafter cited in text.
10. Patricia Neal, *As I Am: An Autobiography* (New York: Simon & Schuster, 1988), 155.
11. Tessa Dahl Kelly, "Gipsy House," *House and Garden,* Jan. 1988, 143–44.
12. Granville Hicks, "Small Handful of the Superb," *Saturday Review,* 20 February 1960, 15.
13. Roald Dahl, "Let's Build a Skyscraper, but Let's Find a Good Book First," *New York Times Book Review,* 1 November 1964, 2; hereafter cited in text as "Let's Build."
14. Alasdair Campbell, "Children's Authors: Roald Dahl," *School Librarian,* June 1981 108–14; hereafter cited in text.

## Chapter Two

1. Roald Dahl, *Over to You* (Middlesex, England: Penguin Books, 1973), 40; hereafter cited in text as *Over*.
2. Peter Lennon, "A Bumpy Ride to Fantasy," *London Times,* 22 December 1983, 8.
3. Roald Dahl, *The Gremlins* (New York: Random House, 1943), n.p.; hereafter cited in text as *Gremlins*.
4. Richard Shale, *Donald Duck Joins Up: The Walt Disney Studio During World War II* (Ann Arbor, Mich.: UMI Research Press, 1982), 81–84. See also John Cawley, "Walt Disney and 'The Gremlins': An Unfinished Story," *American Classic Screen* 4 (Spring 1980): 8–11.
5. E. L. Buell, "Gremlins, Widgets and Fifinellas," *New York Times Book Review,* 13 June 1943, 9.
6. Nona Balakian, "Gremlins—and Mr. Dahl," *New York Times Book Review,* 10 February 1946, 6.
7. Orville Prescott, *Yale Review* 35 (Spring 1946): 575.
8. Michael Straight, "To Whom So Much Was Owed," *Saturday Review,* 9 March 1946, 13.
9. Roald Dahl, *Some Time Never: A Fable for Supermen* (New York: Charles Scribner's Sons, 1948), 112; hereafter cited in text as *Some Time*.
10. Review of *Some Time Never, Kirkus Reviews,* 1 February 1948, 63.
11. Joe McCarthy, review of *Some Time Never, New York Times Book Review,* 20 June 1948, 22.
12. Bergen Evens, "Survivors of World War IV," *Saturday Review,* 3 April 1948, 20.
13. Thomas Hobbes, *Leviathan* (Middlesex, England: Pelican Books, 1968), 186.

## Chapter Three

1. Roald Dahl, *Someone Like You* (New York: Knopf, 1953), 165; hereafter cited in text as *Someone*.
2. James Kelly, "With Waves of Tension," *New York Times Book Review,* 8 November 1953, 5.
3. William Penden, "Collection of Curiosos," *Saturday Review,* 26 December 1953, 15.
4. "British O. Henry," *Time,* 28 December 1953, 59.
5. Roald Dahl, *Kiss Kiss* (New York: Knopf, 1960), 14; hereafter cited in text as *Kiss*.
6. "In Saki's Steps," *Time,* 22 February 1960, 106.

7. Malcolm Bradbury, "Always a Dog Beneath the Skin," *New York Times Book Review,* 7 February 1960, 5.

8. "Sweet and Sour," *Times Literary Supplement,* 28 October 1960, 697.

9. Allan Warren, "Roald Dahl: Nasty, Nasty," in *Discovering Modern Horror Fiction,* ed. Darrell Schweitzer (Mercer Island, Wash.: Starmount House, 1985), 125.

10. Roald Dahl, *Switch Bitch* (New York: Knopf, 1974), 175; hereafter cited in text as *Switch.*

11. J. D. O'Hara, review of *Switch Bitch, New Republic,* 19 October 1974, 23.

12. Richard P. Brickner, "Pain Is the Feature," *New York Times Book Review,* 27 October 1974, 44–45.

13. Charlotte W. Draper, review of *The Wonderful Story of Henry Sugar and Six More, Horn Book,* February 1978, 52–53.

14. Christopher Dickey, "A Dahl for All Seasons," *Washington Post Book World,* 13 November 1978, E1–E2.

15. Sarah Crichton, "PW Interviews: Roald Dahl," *Publishers Weekly,* 6 June 1980, 11.

16. Roald Dahl, *My Uncle Oswald* (New York: Knopf, 1980), 230–31.

17. Lisa Tuttle, "TZ Interview: Roald Dahl," *Twilight Zone,* January/February 1983, 72.

18. Molly Hardwick, review of *My Uncle Oswald, Books and Bookmen,* 3 December 1979, 17.

19. David Cook, review of *My Uncle Oswald, New Statesman,* 23 November 1979, 816.

20. Rhonda Koenig, review of *My Uncle Oswald, New Republic,* 19 April 1980, 37–38.

21. Vance Bourjaily, "Civilized Ribaldry," *New York Times Book Review,* 20 April 1980, 15.

## Chapter Four

1. Roald Dahl, *James and the Giant Peach* (New York: Knopf, 1961), 9; hereafter cited in text as *James.*

2. For more information about splitting, see Mark I. West, "Regression and the Fragmentation of the Self in *James and the Giant Peach," Children's Literature in Education* 16 (Winter 1985): 219–25.

3. Charlotte Jackson, review of *James and the Giant Peach, San Francisco Chronicle,* 10 December 1961, 48.

4. Review of *James and the Giant Peach, Kirkus Reviews,* 15 August 1961, 727.

5. M. S. Libby, review of *James and the Giant Peach, New York Herald Tribune,* 12 November 1961, sec. 12, 14.

6. Ethel L. Heins, review of *James and the Giant Peach, School Library Journal,* November 1961, 50.

7. Kevin Nudd, "The Children's Books of Roald Dahl," *Book and Magazine Collector,* January 1989, 17–18.

8. Roald Dahl, *Charlie and the Chocolate Factory* (New York: Knopf, 1964), 5; hereafter cited in text as *Chocolate.*

9. Charlotte Jackson, review of *Charlie and the Chocolate Factory, Atlantic Monthly,* December 1964, 162.

10. Alice Dalgliesh, review of *Charlie and the Chocolate Factory, Saturday Review,* 7 November 1964, 53.

11. Aileen Pippett, review of *Charlie and the Chocolate Factory, New York Times Book Review,* 25 October 1964, 36.

12. Lois Kalb Bouchard, "A New Look at Old Favorites: *Charlie and the Chocolate Factory,*" in *The Black American in Books for Children: Readings in Racism,* ed. Donnarae MacCann and Gloria Woodard (Metuchen, N.J.: Scarecrow Press, 1972), 112; hereafter cited in text.

13. Mark I. West, *Trust Your Children: Voices Against Censorship in Children's Literature* (New York: Neal-Schuman, 1988), 72; hereafter cited in text.

14. Eleanor Cameron, "McLuhan, Youth, and Literature," *Horn Book,* October 1972, 438; hereafter cited in text.

15. Eleanor Cameron, "A Reply to Roald Dahl," *Horn Book,* April 1973, 128.

16. Eleanor Cameron, "A Question of Taste," *Children's Literature in Education* 7 (Summer 1976): 61; hereafter cited in text.

17. Hamida Bosmajian, "*Charlie and the Chocolate Factory* and Other Excremental Visions," *Lion and the Unicorn* 9 (1985): 36; hereafter cited in text. This article won the Children's Literature Association's award for the best scholarly article about children's literature published in 1985.

18. Roald Dahl, "*Charlie and the Chocolate Factory*: A Reply," *Horn Book,* February 1973, 78.

## *Chapter Five*

1. Roald Dahl, *Charlie and the Great Glass Elevator* (New York: Knopf, 1972), 114; hereafter cited in text as *Glass.*

2. Julia Whedon, review of *Charlie and the Great Glass Elevator, New York Times Book Review,* 17 September 1972, 8.

3. Karla Kuskin, review of *Charlie and the Great Glass Elevator, Saturday Review,* 10 March 1973, 68.

4. Roald Dahl, *Danny, the Champion of the World* (New York: Knopf, 1982), 28; hereafter cited in text as *Danny*.

5. Philippa Pearce, "Forbidden Pleasures," *Times Literary Supplement*, 5 December 1975, 1460.

6. Margery Fisher, review of *Danny the Champion of the World*, *Growing Point*, January 1976, 2799.

7. Roald Dahl, *George's Marvelous Medicine* (New York: Knopf, 1982), 2; hereafter cited in text as *George*.

8. Nicholas Tucker, "Inventing for Fun," *Times Literary Supplement*, 24 July 1981, 839.

9. "For Immediate Disposal," *Economist*, 26 December 1981, 108.

10. David Rees, "Dahl's Chickens," *Children's Literature in Education* 19 (Fall 1988): 149; hereafter cited in text.

11. Charles Gerard Van Renen, "A Critical Review of Some of Roald Dahl's Books for Children, with Particular Reference to a 'Subversive' Element in His Writing" (master's thesis, Rhodes University, 1985), 19.

12. Roald Dahl, *The BFG* (New York: Farrar, Straus & Giroux, 1982), 45; hereafter cited in text as *BFG*.

13. Judith Elkin, review of *The BFG, Times Literary Supplement*, 26 November 1982, 1303.

14. Gillian Avery, review of *The BFG, Spectator*, 4 December 1982, 26.

15. Ruth Gordon, review of *The BFG, New York Times Book Review*, 9 January 1983, 32.

16. Roald Dahl, *The Witches* (New York: Farrar, Straus & Giroux, 1983), 37; hereafter cited in text as *Witches*.

17. See, for example, Catherine Itzin, "Bewitching the Boys," *Times Educational Supplement*, 27 December 1985, 13.

18. Sally Brompton, "Black Looks at the Littlest Books," *London Times*, 24 November 1986, 15.

19. Walter Clemons, "Christmas Treats," *Newsweek*, 5 December 1983, 111.

20. Nancy C. Hammond, review of *The Witches, Horn Book*, April 1984, 194.

21. Erica Jong, "The Boy Who Became a Mouse," *New York Times Book Review*, 13 November 1983, 45.

22. Roald Dahl, *Matilda* (New York: Viking Kestrel, 1988), 66–67; hereafter cited in text as *Matilda*.

23. Vicki Weissman, review of *Matilda, New York Times Book Review*, 15 January 1989, 31.

24. Linda Taylor, review of *Matilda, Times Literary Supplement*, 6 May 1988, 513.

## Chapter Six

1. Roald Dahl, *The Magic Finger* (New York: Harper & Row, 1966), 4; hereafter cited in text as *Magic.*

2. Alice Dalgliesh, "That Pointing Finger," *Saturday Review,* 17 September 1966, 40–41.

3. Roald Dahl, *Fantastic Mr. Fox* (New York: Knopf, 1970), 15; hereafter cited in text as *Fox.*

4. Margery Fisher, review of *Fantastic Mr. Fox, Growing Point,* April 1971, 1716.

5. Ingeborg Boudreau, "Fable and Fantasy," *New York Times Book Review,* 8 November 1970, 48.

6. Review of *Fantastic Mr. Fox, Publishers Weekly,* 2 November 1970, 53.

7. Roald Dahl, *The Enormous Crocodile* (New York: Knopf, 1978), n.p.; hereafter cited in text as *Crocodile.*

8. Elaine Moss, "Going to the Pictures," *Times Literary Supplement,* 29 September 1978, 1087.

9. Elizabeth Jane Howard, "Salad Days," *New Statesman,* 3 November 1978, 591–92.

10. Georgess McHargue, review of *The Enormous Crocodile, New York Times Book Review,* 10 December 1978, 94.

11. Virginia Haviland, review of *The Enormous Crocodile, Horn Book,* April 1979, 94.

12. Roald Dahl, *The Twits* (New York: Knopf, 1981), 7; hereafter cited in text as *Twits.*

13. Roald Dahl, "Smoked Cheese," *Atlantic Monthly,* November 1945, 115.

14. Paul E. McGhee, *Humor: Its Origin and Development* (San Francisco: W. H. Freeman, 1979), 80.

15. Martha Wolfenstein, *Children's Humor: A Psychological Analysis* (Bloomington: Indiana University Press, 1978), 45.

16. Karla Kuskin, review of *The Twits, New York Times Book Review,* 29 March 1981, 38.

17. Gillian Cross, review of *The Twits, Times Literary Supplement,* 21 November 1980, 1330.

18. Charles Sarland, "*The Secret Seven* vs *The Twits:* Cultural Clash or Cosy Combination?" *Signal,* September 1983, 162.

19. Review of *The Giraffe and the Pelly and Me, Economist,* 30 November 1985, 89.

20. Ann A. Flowers, review of *The Giraffe and the Pelly and Me, Horn Book,* January 1986, 46.

21. Susan Scheps, review of *The Giraffe and the Pelly and Me,* *School Library Journal,* December 1985, 69.

22. Roald Dahl, "Writing Children's Books," *The Writer,* August 1976, 19.

23. Roald Dahl, *Esio Trot* (New York: Viking, 1990), 23; hereafter cited in text as *Esio.*

24. Review of *Esio Trot, Publishers Weekly,* 9 November 1990, 58.

25. Roald Dahl, *The Minpins* (London: Jonathan Cape, 1991), n.p.

## Chapter Seven

1. Roald Dahl, *The Giraffe and the Pelly and Me* (New York: Farrar, Straus & Giroux, 1985), n.p.; hereafter cited in text as *Giraffe.*

2. Roald Dahl, *Roald Dahl's Revolting Rhymes* (New York: Knopf, 1983), 10; hereafter cited in text as *Revolting.*

3. Trev Jones, review of *Roald Dahl's Revolting Rhymes, School Library Journal,* April 1983, 112.

4. Thomas M. Disch, "Beyond Mother Goose," *Washington Post Book World,* 8 May 1983, 13–14.

5. Andrew Hislop, "Earthy Couplets," *Times Literary Supplement,* 23 July 1982, 793.

6. Roald Dahl, *Dirty Beasts* (New York: Farrar, Straus & Giroux, 1983), n.p.; hereafter cited in text as *Dirty.*

7. Review of *Dirty Beasts, Economist,* 26 November 1983, 98.

8. Maria Salvadore, review of *Dirty Beasts, School Library Journal,* August 1974, 71.

9. Candida Lycett Green, "Little Shockers," *Times Literary Supplement,* 22 July 1983, 779.

10. Roald Dahl, *Rhyme Stew* (New York: Viking, 1990), 23; hereafter cited in text as *Stew.*

11. Francelia Butler, *Skipping Around the World: The Ritual Nature of Folk Rhymes* (New York: Ballantine Books, 1989), 50.

12. Patricia Dooley, review of *Rhyme Stew, Library Journal,* 1 May 1990, 90.

13. Review of *Rhyme Stew, Publishers Weekly,* 9 February 1990, 58.

14. D. J. Enright, "Unangelic Aspects," *Times Literary Supplement,* 24 November 1989, 1310.

15. Mary Smith, "Several Jokes too Many," *London Times,* 27 September 1989, 19.

*Chapter Eight*

1. Michael Rosen, review of *Boy: Tales of Childhood, New Statesman,* 21 December 1984.

2. Ann A. Flowers, review of *Boy: Tales of Childhood, Horn Book,* March 1985, 190.

3. Gahan Wilson, review of *Going Solo, New York Times Book Review,* 12 October 1986, 12.

4. Ann A. Flowers, review of *Going Solo, Horn Book,* January 1987, 190.

# Selected Bibliography

## Primary Works

### Collections of Short Stories

*Ah, Sweet Mystery of Life*. London: Michael Joseph, 1989.
*The Best of Roald Dahl*. New York: Vintage Books, 1978.
*Completely Unexpected Tales*. Middlesex, England: Penguin Books, 1986.
*Kiss Kiss*. New York: Knopf, 1960; London: Michael Joseph, 1960.
*More Tales of the Unexpected*. London: Michael Joseph, 1980.
*Over to You: Ten Stories of Flyers and Flying*. New York: Reynal & Hitchcock, 1945; Middlesex, England: Penguin Books, 1973.
*The Roald Dahl Omnibus*. New York: Dorset Press, 1986.
*Selected Stories of Roald Dahl*. New York: Modern Library, 1968.
*Someone Like You*. New York: Knopf, 1953; London: Secker & Warburg, 1954.
*Switch Bitch*. New York: Knopf, 1974; London: Michael Joseph, 1974.
*Tales of the Unexpected*. New York: Vintage Books, 1979.
*Twenty-six Kisses from Roald Dahl*. London: Michael Joseph, 1969.
*Two Fables*. Middlesex, England: Viking Penguin, 1986.
*The Wonderful Story of Henry Sugar and Six More*. New York: Knopf, 1977; London: Jonathan Cape, 1977.

### Novels for Adults

*My Uncle Oswald*. London: Michael Joseph, 1979; New York: Knopf, 1980.
*Some Time Never: A Fable for Supermen*. New York: Charles Scribner's Sons, 1948.

### Novels and Story Books for Children

*The BFG*. London: Jonathan Cape, 1982; New York: Farrar, Straus & Giroux, 1982.

*Charlie and the Chocolate Factory.* New York: Knopf, 1964, (rev. ed., 1973); London: Allen & Unwin, 1967.

*Charlie and the Great Glass Elevator.* New York: Knopf, 1972; London: Allen & Unwin, 1973.

*Danny, the Champion of the World.* New York: Knopf, 1975; London: Jonathan Cape, 1975.

*The Enormous Crocodile.* London: Jonathan Cape, 1978; New York: Knopf, 1978.

*Esio Trot.* London: Jonathan Cape, 1990; New York: Viking, 1990.

*Fantastic Mr. Fox.* New York: Knopf, 1970; London: Allen & Unwin, 1970.

*George's Marvellous Medicine.* London: Jonathan Cape, 1981.

*George's Marvelous Medicine.* New York: Knopf, 1982.

*The Giraffe and the Pelly and Me.* London: Jonathan Cape, 1985; New York: Farrar, Straus & Giroux, 1985.

*The Gremlins.* New York: Random House, 1943. London: Collins, 1944.

*James and the Giant Peach.* New York: Knopf, 1961; London: Allen & Unwin, 1967.

*The Magic Finger.* New York: Harper & Row, 1966; London: Allen & Unwin, 1970.

*Matilda.* London: Jonathan Cape, 1988; New York: Viking Kestrel, 1988.

*The Minpins.* London: Jonathan Cape, 1991; New York: Viking, 1991.

*The Twits.* London: Jonathan Cape, 1980; New York: Knopf, 1981.

*The Vicar of Nibbleswicke.* London: Jonathan Cape, 1991; New York: Viking, 1992.

*The Witches.* London: Jonathan Cape, 1983; New York: Farrar, Straus & Giroux, 1983.

## Collections of Verse

*Dirty Beasts.* London: Jonathan Cape, 1983; New York: Farrar, Straus & Giroux, 1983.

*Rhyme Stew.* London: Jonathan Cape, 1989; New York: Viking, 1990.

*Roald Dahl's Revolting Rhymes.* London: Jonathan Cape, 1982; New York: Knopf, 1983.

## Autobiographies

*Boy: Tales of Childhood.* London: Jonathan Cape, 1984; New York: Farrar, Straus & Giroux, 1984.

*Going Solo.* London: Jonathan Cape, 1986; New York: Farrar, Straus & Giroux, 1986.

**Edited Work**

*Roald Dahl's Book of Ghost Stories.* London: Jonathan Cape, 1983; New York: Farrar, Straus & Giroux, 1983.

**Miscellaneous Publications**

*Memories with Food at Gipsy House.* Co-authored with Felicity Dahl. Middlesex, England: Viking, 1991.
*The Dahl Diary 1992.* Middlesex, England: Puffin Books, 1991.

## Secondary Works

**Biographies**

**Powling, Chris.** *Roald Dahl.* Middlesex, England: Puffin Books, 1985. A short biography intended for children.
**Farrell, Barry.** *Pat and Roald.* New York: Random House, 1969. Focuses on the relationship between Dahl and Patricia Neal following her stroke in 1967 but also provides an overview of Dahl's life.

**Interviews**

**Tuttle, Lisa.** "TZ Interview: Roald Dahl." *Twilight Zone Magazine,* January 1983, 70–73. Focuses on Dahl's adult fiction and his views on contemporary literature.
**West, Mark I.** "Interview with Roald Dahl." *Children's Literature in Education* 21 (June 1990): 61–66. Covers Dahl's career as a children's author and his views on children's literature.
**West, Mark I.** *Trust Your Children: Voices Against Censorship in Children's Literature.* New York: Neal Schuman, 1988. Contains a brief interview in which Dahl discusses the controversies surrounding some of his children's books.
**Wintle, Justin, and Emma Fisher.** *The Pied Pipers: Interviews with the Influential Creators of Children's Literature.* New York: Paddington Press, 1974. Contains a wide-ranging interview in which Dahl discusses his early writing career, his beginnings as a children's author, and his experiences in the film industry.

## Critical Studies

**Bosmajian, Hamida.** "*Charlie and the Chocolate Factory* and Other Excremental Visions." *Lion and the Unicorn* 9 (1985): 36–49. Argues that *Charlie and the Chocolate Factory* makes extensive use of excremental imagery and compares the book to other works that use this type of imagery, including Dante's *Inferno* and Swift's *Gulliver's Travels.*

**Bouchard, Lois Kalb.** "A New Look at Old Favorites: *Charlie and the Chocolate Factory.* In *The Black American in Books for Children: Readings in Racism,* edited by Donnarae MacCann and Gloria Woodard, 112–15. Metuchen, N.J.: Scarecrow Press, 1972. Argues that the first edition of *Charlie and the Chocolate Factory* is racist.

**Cameron, Eleanor.** "McLuhan, Youth and Literature." *Horn Book,* October 1972, 433–40. Contains a sharp attack on *Charlie and the Chocolate Factory* in which Cameron accuses the book of encouraging sadism.

**Cameron, Eleanor.** "A Question of Taste: A Reply to Anne Merrick." *Children's Literature in Education* 21 (Summer 1976): 59–63. Criticizes Merrick for suggesting that teachers should read *Charlie and the Chocolate Factory* to their classes.

**Campbell, Alasdair.** "Children's Writers: 6 Roald Dahl." *School Librarian,* June 1981, 108–14. Analyzes several of Dahl's children's books and concludes that most of them are superior works of literature.

**Chesterfield-Evans, Jan.** "Roald Dahl: A Discussion and Comparison of His Stories for Children and Adults." *Orana* 19 (November 1983): 165–68. Compares *Danny, the Champion of the World* to Dahl's adult story entitled "The Champion of the World."

**Culley, Jonathon.** "Roald Dahl—It's About Children and It's for Children—But Is it Suitable?" *Children's Literature in Education* 22 (March 1991): 59–73. Examines the controversy surrounding several of Dahl's children's books.

**Merrick, Anne.** "*The Nightwatchmen* and *Charlie and the Chocolate Factory* as Books to Be Read to Children: Children's Responses in Conflict with Adult Judgement." *Children's Literature in Education* 16 (Summer 1975): 21–30. Expresses reservations about the violence in *Charlie and the Chocolate Factory* but argues that teachers should still read the book to their classes.

**Nudd, Kevin.** "The Children's Books of Roald Dahl." *Book and Magazine Collector,* January 1989, 12–19. Summarizes the publishing history of several of Dahl's children's books.

**Rees, David.** "Dahl's Chickens: Roald Dahl." *Children's Literature in Education* 19 (1988): 143–55. Examines most of Dahl's children's books and argues that they convey conflicting moral messages.

**Sarland, Charles.** "*The Secret Seven* vs *The Twits*: Cultural Clash or Cosy Combination?" *Signal* 42 (September 1983): 155–71. Analyzes the narrative structure and ideological aspects of *The Twits* and concludes that the book is more complex than it first appears to be.

**Warren, Alan.** "Roald Dahl: Nasty, Nasty." In *Discovering Modern Horror Fiction,* edited by Darrell Schweitzer, 120–28. Mercer Island, Wash.: Starmont House, 1985. Provides an overview of Dahl's macabre short stories.

**West, Mark I.** "The Grotesque and the Taboo in Roald Dahl's Humorous Writings for Children." *Children's Literature Association Quarterly* 15 (Fall 1990): 115–16. Analyzes the use of humor in *The Twits* and *George's Marvelous Medicine.*

**West, Mark I.** "Regression and the Fragmentation of the Self in *James and the Giant Peach.*" *Children's Literature in Education* 16 (Winter 1985): 219–25. Interprets *James and the Giant Peach* from a psychoanalytic perspective.

**Wood, Michael.** "The Confidence Man." *New Society,* 27 December 1979, 14–16. Argues that Dahl is a master at manipulating his readers.

# Index

# The Author

Mark I. West was born in Denver and grew up in the mountains of Colorado. After graduating from Franconia College in Franconia, New Hampshire, he moved to Madison, Wisconsin, where he worked as a preschool teacher and puppeteer. He received his master's degree from the University of Wisconsin–Green Bay and earned a Ph.D. in American Culture from Bowling Green State University in Ohio. He is currently an associate professor of English at the University of North Carolina at Charlotte, where he teaches children's literature. In addition to numerous articles, he has written the books *Children, Culture, and Controversy* and *Trust Your Children: Voices Against Censorship in Children's Literature.* He has also edited *Before Oz: Juvenile Fantasy Stories from Nineteenth-Century America.*